Julio Cortázar

Twayne's World Authors Series
Latin American Literature

David W. Foster, Editor
Arizona State University

TWAS 816

Julio Cortázar lecturing at the University of Oklahoma in Norman, Oklahoma, November 1975. *Photograph by Gil Jain, courtesy of World Literature Today.*

Julio Cortázar

By Terry J. Peavler

Penn State University

Twayne Publishers
A Division of G. K. Hall & Co. • *Boston*

Julio Cortázar
Terry J. Peavler
Copyright 1990 by G. K. Hall & Co.
All rights reserved.
Published by Twayne Publishers
A Division of G. K. Hall & Co.
70 Lincoln Street
Boston, Massachusetts 02111

Copyediting supervised by Barbara Sutton
Book production by Janet Z. Reynolds
Book design by Barbara Anderson

Typeset in 11 pt. Garamond
by Compositors Corporation, Cedar Rapids, Iowa

Printed on permanent/durable acid-free paper
and bound in the United States of America

First published 1990.
10 9 8 7 6 5 4 3 2 1

Library of Congress Cataloging-in-Publication Data

Peavler, Terry J., 1942–
    Julio Cortázar / by Terry J. Peavler.
        p.   cm. — (Twayne's world authors series ; TWAS 816. Latin
American literature)
    Includes bibliographical references.
    ISBN 0-8057-8257-5 (alk. paper).
    1. Cortázar, Julio—Criticism and interpretation.   I. Title.
II. Series: Twayne's world authors series ; TWAS 816.   III. Series:
Twayne's world authors series.   Latin American literature.
PQ7797.C7145Z738   1990
863–dc20   89-38926
                                                                        CIP

For Louise Peavler Bosler

Contents

About the Author

Terry J. Peavler received his Ph.D. in comparative literature from the University of California in 1973. He is currently professor of Spanish and Comparative Literature at Penn State University, where he has taught courses on Spanish American literature, literary theory, and comparative literature since 1971. He has published numerous articles on these subjects in *Hispania, Hispanófila, Latin American Literary Review, Latin American Research Review, PMLA, Revista de Estudios Hispánicos,* and other scholarly journals, and he has also published a study of the novel as a literary genre, *Individuations: The Novel as Dissent* (Landover, Md.: University Press of America, 1987) and an analysis of the fiction of the Mexican writer, Juan Rulfo, *El texto en llamas: el arte narrativo de Juan Rulfo,* University of Texas Series in Contemporary Spanish-American Fiction (New York: Peter Lang, 1988).

Preface

At the time of his death on 12 February 1984, Julio Cortázar left a legacy of over thirty volumes of essays, poems, plays, and some of the most brilliant prose fiction written during the twentieth century. The significance of his achievement is reflected in the vast number of scholarly books and articles that have been dedicated to his work. Although best known as the author of *Rayuela (Hopscotch)*, an iconoclastic novel that sent shockwaves through the international literary establishment in 1963, his greatest aesthetic achievements may well have come in the area of the short story, a form that he mastered.

The present study offers an overview of Cortázar's work, with special emphasis on those writings that have received relatively less attention. Several such works are treated in the first chapter, from the early, poetic *Los reyes* (The monarchs) through the plays and other writings that were published posthumously. In addition, Cortázar's problematic stance *vis-à-vis* art and revolution is examined at some length in this same chapter. Because of Cortázar's excellence and prolificacy as an author of short stories, a full four chapters are devoted to that genre, with discussions and analyses of more than eighty stories. The novels are examined together, in chapter 6, and the famous potpourri books in chapter 7.

As this study goes to press, it provides the most comprehensive treatment of Julio Cortázar's writings. Space requirements have made it necessary to limit the discussion of some works, particularly the novels. Consequently, I have endeavored, except when required for the sake of clarity, not to rehash arguments that have already been amply treated elsewhere. Every year one or more previously unpublished manuscripts by Cortázar find their way into print, and new critical studies appear, it seems, almost weekly. Consequently, as is always the case, any critical study, particularly one that seeks to be comprehensive, is out of date before it even goes to press. I have included a few book-length studies that I was unable to consult in the bibliography, but Cortázar's *Divertimento* (Amusement), a prose work of 126 pages, deserves mention here. It was apparently written in 1949, which would make it roughly contemporary with *Los reyes* (The monarchs). It is probably, like the author's early novel *El examen* (The exam), of interest only to specialists.

Whenever possible, I have used existing English translations followed by standard references. For untranslated works, I have provided my own transla-tions without quotation marks and without comment. In a few instances, when existing translations are not acceptable, I have supplied my own version followed by the notation "my translation." Finally, for essays, interviews and other texts that are cited for content, not style or aesthetics, I have given only my translations, followed by references to the original.

I am deeply grateful to Iliana Sánchez Ramírez for her assistance in obtain-ing materials for this study and to David William Foster for his invaluable comments on the manuscript. The photograph of Julio Cortázar at the Uni-versity of Oklahoma was provided by *World Literature Today.*

Terry J. Peavler

Penn State University

Chronology

1914 Julio Cortázar born 26 August in Brussels.

1918 Family moves to Banfield, a suburb of Buenos Aires.

1926 Julio begins studies at Escuela Normal Mariano Acosta in Buenos Aires.

1932 Earns degree as public school teacher.

1935 Begins college classes at the University of Buenos Aires.

1937 Accepts high school teaching post in Buenos Aires Province.

1938 First book, *Presencia*, a collection of sonnets, published under pseudonym Julio Denis.

1940 Essay on Rimbaud in the important literary magazine *Huella* also published under the name of Julio Denis.

1944 Begins to teach course on Rimbaud, Mallarmé, and Keats at the University of Cuyo in Mendoza.

1946 Forced to give up academic career because of political (anti-Peronista) activities. Essay on John Keats and his first major short story, "Casa tomada" ("House Taken Over"), published.

1947 Receives degree as a public translator.

1949 *Los reyes* (The monarchs), a highly poetic drama on the Minotaur, published.

1951 Goes to Paris on a scholarship. Translates Louisa May Alcott's *Little Women* into Spanish. First major collection of short stories, *Bestiario* (Bestiary), published in Buenos Aires.

1952 Begins working as a UNESCO translator, a job he continued throughout his life.

1953 Establishes permanent residency in Paris. Marries Aurora Bernández. Brief residence in Rome. Translates Edgar Allan Poe's prose works into Spanish.

1956 Second major collection of stories, *Final del juego (End of the*

Game), published in Mexico; *Obras en prosa*, translation of Poe's works, also published.

1959   Third major story collection, *Las armas secretas* (Secret weapons), published.

1960   Visits the United States for the first time. First novel (although not the first he had written), *Los premios (The Winners)*, published.

1962   *Historias de cronopios y de famas (Cronopios and Famas)*.

1963   *Rayuela (Hopscotch)*. Visits Cuba, and becomes far more visible politically.

1964   Second version of *Final del juego (End of the Game)* published in Buenos Aires, with ten additional short stories, his fourth major collection.

1966   Fifth major story collection, *Todos los fuegos el fuego (All Fires the Fire)*, and Gregory Rabassa's English translation of his novel *Hopscotch* published. Michelangelo Antonioni makes the film *Blow-up*, based on his short story "Las babas del diablo."

1967   *La vuelta al día en ochenta mundos (Around the Day in Eighty Worlds)*, his first major collection of miscellanea, published.

1968   Third novel, *62. modelo para armar (62: A Model Kit)*, published.

1969   *Ultimo round* (Final round), his second major collection of miscellanea, published.

1970   Visits Chile. First complete story collection published.

1971   *Pameos y meopas* (Peoms and meops), a collection of poems, published.

1972   The very lyrical *Prosa del observatorio* (Prose from the observatory) published.

1973   Returns to Buenos Aires for the publication of fourth novel, *Libro de Manuel (A Manual for Manuel)*.

1974   *Octaedro* (Octahedron), his sixth major collection of stories, published. Visits New York for P.E.N. translation congress.

1975   Attends session of the International Commission to Investigate the Crimes of the Military Junta in Chile. Is honored at the Oklahoma Conference on Writers of the Hispanic World.

Proceedings of conference published in special issue of *Books Abroad* 50, no. 3 (Summer 1976).

1976 Visits Cuba and Nicaragua.

1977 Seventh story collection, *Alguien que anda por ahí* (Someone walking around), published. Continues travels.

1978 *Territorios* (Territories), a book on art, published.

1979 *Un tal Lucas (A Certain Lucas),* published. Becomes involved in the Russell Tribunal investigating crimes against peoples of Latin America.

1980 Eighth major collection of stories, *Queremos tanto a Glenda (We Love Glenda So Much),* published. Participates in special symposium on Julio Cortázar at Barnard College.

1981 Becomes French citizen.

1982 His companion, Carol Dunlop, dies. Ninth collection of stories, *Deshoras* (Bad timing), published.

1983 *Nicaragua tan violentamente dulce* (Nicaragua, so violently sweet) and *Los autonautas del cosmopista* (The autonauts of the cosmopike), both written with Carol Dunlop, published. After visit to Cuba goes to New York to address the United Nations concerning the "disappeared" in Latin America.

1984 Dies 12 February of leukemia and heart disease in Saint Lazare hospital in Paris at age sixty-nine. Buried in Montparnasse cemetery.

Chapter One
Julio Cortázar:
An Overview

Julio Florencio Cortázar was born to Argentine parents, María Scott and Julio Cortázar, in Brussels, Belgium, on 26 August 1914. Four years later, with their child already fluent in French, the Cortázars moved to Banfield, a suburb of Buenos Aires. This neighborhood Julio would call home throughout his adolescence and early adulthood, and it would provide the setting for many of his writings.

Young Julio attended school in Buenos Aires and in 1932 was certified as a primary and secondary school teacher. After one year of studies at the University of Buenos Aires, he began teaching high school in Bolívar and Chivilcoy, towns in the province of Buenos Aires. In 1938 he published a collection of poems, *Presencia* (Presence),[1] and three years later the prose work "Rimbaud,"[2] both under the pseudonym Julio Denis.

In 1944 Cortázar was hired to teach literature at the University of Cuyo, in Mendoza, where he later became involved in demonstrations against Juan Domingo Perón, who soon would become president of Argentina. Arrested for his activities, and recognizing that his dismissal was imminent, he resigned his position and returned to Buenos Aires, where he managed a publishing association, the Cámara Argentina del Libro. Also in 1946, Jorge Luis Borges, then editor of the literary journal *Anales de Buenos Aires*, published Cortázar's famous "Casa tomada" ("House Taken Over"),[3] thus making it the first story Cortázar published, although it was far from being the first he had written.

Through incredibly hard work Cortázar managed not only to fulfill his obligations at the Cámara Argentina del Libro but also to complete the requirements for a degree in public translation in a scant few months. While this accomplishment left him exhausted, it also produced in him a number of temporary neuroses that provided the inspiration for some of his classic stories, and allowed him to leave the Cámara Argentina del Libro to become a full-time translator.

During this period Cortázar published *Los reyes* (The monarchs, 1949),[4] a

1

book that met with almost total silence in Argentina. In 1951 he published his translation of Louisa May Alcott's *Little Women*[5] and the first book-length collection of his own short stories, *Bestiario* (Bestiary),[6] which quickly gained him a reputation as an excellent writer of short fiction.

Also in 1951 Cortázar took up residence in France, taking advantage of a government scholarship to study in Paris. Although he would travel widely, and in his later years with some frequency, especially to Argentina, Cuba, Nicaragua, and the United States, France was to be his home for the rest of his life. There he worked as a translator for UNESCO, eventually dividing his time between a summer home in Saignon and a small Parisian apartment. In 1981 he was granted the French citizenship that he had long sought. Nonetheless, he always thought of himself as Argentine, and in fact would not have petitioned for French citizenship if it were not legally possible to be a citizen of both countries.

Cortázar married for the first time in 1953, at the age of thirty-nine. His first wife, Aurora Bernández, collaborated in his translation of the complete prose works of Edgar Allan Poe, while the couple was living in Rome.[7] This important work, as well as Cortázar's second major collection of stories, *Final del juego* (End of the game),[8] was published in 1956, followed only three years later by a third collection of stories, *Las armas secretas* (Secret weapons).[9]

From the fifties on, Julio Cortázar published a steady stream of literature of the highest quality—over eighty short stories, five novels, four major miscellanies, two books of poetry, two plays, countless essays, prose poems, and travelogues. During his lifetime he was recognized as one of the most important creative writers of the twentieth century, and yet for most of his life he continued to work as a free-lance translator, preferring not to think of himself as a professional author.

While he was a private man who had a greater liking for the company of a few close friends than the attention of his countless admirers, he traveled widely, not only to the Americas, but to India and throughout Europe. He made his final trip to New York in 1983 to address a United Nations Commission on International Humanitarian Issues. Although many of his travels are documented in his writings, the most memorable, at least for his readers, are the first visit to Nicaragua, powerfully rendered in his "Apocalipsis de Solentiname" ("Apocalypse at Solentiname")[10] and the strange, touching, *Los autonautas de la cosmopista* (The autonauts of the cosmopike),[11] which documents a journey that he undertook in 1982 with his companion and collaborator, Carol Dunlop, along the turnpike from Paris to Marseille. Less than six months after the conclusion of this unusual voyage Dunlop died of leukemia, and on 12 February 1984 Cortázar too succumbed to leukemia and heart disease. He was sixty-nine.

Julio Cortázar was an extremely tall (six feet four inches), raw-boned man. Despite his relatively poor health as a child, until the last few years of his life, when his health declined rapidly, he looked to be easily twenty years younger than his actual age. During his childhood he was less active and healthy than many of his friends, so he turned to literature and to music for entertainment. He read voraciously and wrote voluminously, even as a child, but he was a perfectionist who refused to publish his early writings. In fact, he was thirty-one when "Casa tomada" ("House Taken Over") was published, and thirty-seven when *Bestiario* finally began to bring him a reputation as a writer. His meticulous attention to the details of his craft (he claims to have burned the 600-page manuscript of an early novel) shows clearly in the extremely high quality of almost all of his published work.

His taste in literature tended toward the fantastic and the mysterious, especially as a child, and as a young adult he was influenced by the surrealists. Despite strong political differences with his early mentor, Jorge Luis Borges, the dean of Argentine letters, Cortázar never failed to acknowledge his admiration for that superb craftsman of the short story, the genre that Cortázar himself mastered. As an adult, Cortázar came under the spell, perhaps through Borges, of oriental mysticism, especially Zen Buddhism and the Vedanta. In music, his preference was for classical and jazz, particularly improvisational jazz ("cool" not "hot"), and although he frequently pointed out the relative poverty of Argentina's own tango when compared to jazz, he nonetheless helped write tangos in his later years, and even collaborated in opening a tango parlor in Paris—Les Trottoirs de Buenos Aires (The sidewalks of Buenos Aires)—in 1981.

Among Latin American writers, Cortázar preferred, along with Borges, whom he credited with teaching him how to use language forcefully and economically,[12] Mario Vargas Llosa, Gabriel García Márquez, Carlos Fuentes, fellow Argentine Leopoldo Marechal (although he disagreed with him violently on politics), and Juan Rulfo. He disliked most Spanish prose authors, particularly those of the twentieth century, but admired many contemporary Spanish poets, including Aleixandre, Salinas, Cernuda, Lorca, and Alberti.[13]

Despite his enduring love for jazz, he felt that the masterpieces of classical music, the compositions of Mozart, Beethoven, Bartok, and Stravinsky, are like the great classics of literature, "the greatest achievements possible in music."[14] Jazz held him in its spell because it is based on feelings, not logic, and because it has no final, fixed, "correct" form. The tango, like classical music, is composed, written down, and allows little room for improvisation. Nonetheless, near the end of his life, he pointed out that he did not wish to imply that the tango was inferior, simply that it was a totally different musical form.[15]

Jazz attracted Cortázar because of its freedom, and because of its frequent playfulness, characteristics he also found in Zen Buddhism: "I detest solemn searches. . . . What I like above all about the masters of Zen is their complete lack of solemnity. The deepest insights sometimes emerge from a joke, a gag, or a slap in the face."[16] Surrealism lost its appeal when it became a literary movement instead of an attitude, when it became solemn. This dislike for seriousness explains, in part, his rejection of many Spanish authors: "one of the worst legacies left us by the Spanish is their tendency toward seriousness."[17]

These major events and experiences in Julio Cortázar's life, these tastes, likes, dislikes, and interests, are all reflected clearly in his writings. The Buenos Aires/Paris connection is a recurring motif in countless short stories and reaches its fullest exploration in what many critics and he himself considered his greatest literary achievement, the radically experimental novel, *Rayuela* (*Hopscotch*),[18] first published in 1963. Until the late 1970s, when his stories began to take on a more somber tone, the bulk of his writings were imbued with a sense of playfulness, of good humor, even in the darkest moments.

"Lo lúdico" (The ludic) provides a constant theme in his literature and in his conversations, not only as a sense of humor and of play, but in the sense of the game, an arbitrary though often elaborate set of rules that control our actions. This concept, while often portrayed in Cortázar's works in the guise of children's games, also stretches into adulthood, and frequently takes on extremely serious overtones. Cortázar himself wrote one of his major novels, *62. Modelo para armar* (*62: A Model Kit*),[19] by rigidly adhering to a set of guidelines for a new type of novel that he had first set forth in chapter 62 of *Hopscotch*, the title deriving from that chapter number. Even though he often despaired at the impossibility of the task he had set for himself, he refused to abandon the rules of the game and viewed the novel's completion as one of his proudest achievements. One of his highly acclaimed stories is entitled "Final del juego" ("End of the Game"), and even the motor trip that resulted in *Los autonautas de la cosmopista* was carefully planned and completed according to a set of inviolable, yet purely arbitrary rules.

The travelers, Cortázar and Dunlop, both suffering from leukemia, were required (by their own rules) to take a full thirty days to complete the 800-kilometer drive from Marseille to Paris, along the Southern Turnpike. Furthermore, they were obligated to stop at exactly two rest stops per day, with an obligatory overnight stay at the second, regardless of whether it contained a hotel or was simply a narrow pull-off. Under no circumstances were they allowed to leave the turnpike; friends replenished their store of food and water at designated intervals. Their vehicle was an aging Volkswagen microbus camper—purchased from American poet and translator Paul Blackburn— supplied with food, clothing, and, of course, two typewriters with plenty of paper. Both writers contributed to the chronicle of their voyage, but Julio himself was forced to provide the finishing touches after Dunlop's death.

Los autonautas is not a great work of literature, but it reveals a good deal about Julio Cortázar, for here, long after his commitment to the revolutions in Cuba and Nicaragua, after writing many somber stories portraying violence, cruelty, and even torture, knowing that Carol had but a few months to live and that he too was dying of cancer, he showed that he had never lost his sense of humor or his desire to play what surely seemed to many an infantile game. He himself was proud that he had never lost his childishness, his ability not to take life or literature too seriously.

This attitude may explain, in part, why Cortázar never considered himself a professional writer, for such a self-image might have turned writing into a chore rather than a pleasure. Néstor García Canclini, in a fine analysis of the anthropological bases for Cortázar's writings, has pointed out that "the scant attention paid to work in Cortázar's literature is underscored by the importance given to play."[20] This is not to say that he did not take life or literature seriously, but that he considered both to be too serious to approach without a sense of humor. He was thus able to face the most difficult of times with his characteristic verve, and solve the thorniest of literary problems.

Cortázar often suggested that his vocation as translator not only provided him with material for his stories and opportunities to travel and become involved in world affairs, but that it made him a better writer. He believed, for example, that young writers who are experiencing difficulty with their style should stop writing and translate good literature, for translating the work of great artists would help them find their own way.[21]

As for himself, he claimed that he was drawn to literature merely through avocation: "I shall consider myself until my death an amateur, one who writes because he feels like it, but I have no notion of literary professionalism."[22] Moreover, he was not concerned with producing great literature: "The truth is that I don't care a straw for Literature with a capital L; the only thing that interests me is searching for (and sometimes finding) myself in a contest with words that eventually produces a thing called a book."[23] Even if one ignores all the translations, the combined collections, and many of the works written in collaboration, these "contests" yielded over thirty "books" during his lifetime and several more posthumous volumes.

To study the writings of Julio Cortázar is to expose oneself to the work of one of the twentieth century's great literary artists. The richness and the diversity are dazzling, as is the sheer volume. No single study as brief as mine can possibly do justice to it all. Indeed, the best bibliography on Cortázar, published in 1985,[24] contains over 2,600 entries of primary and secondary sources, and that bibliography is by now far out of date. Nonetheless, Cortázar is best known for his novels and short stories, and these, along with four titles that can hardly be placed in any existing literary category, are the major focus of this study.

Even so, certain works, though not of the main Cortázar canon, cannot be ignored. These include *Los autonautas de la cosmopista*, already described; the very early work, *Los reyes* (1949); two plays, both published posthumously; the collections of poetry; and three highly poetic texts, *Prosa del observatorio* (Prose from the observatory, 1972), *Territorios* (Territories, 1978), and *Silvalandia* (Silvaland, 1984).

Los reyes was always one of Julio Cortázar's favorite works, although it met with little critical success. In fact, many commentators have evidently not consulted the work, but rather have taken the author's word that it is a dramatic poem. While it is composed in dramatic form, and while it is highly poetic, it is written in prose. It is based on the classical legend of the Minotaur, half-bull, half-human, trapped in a labyrinth by King Minos, and fed by an annual sacrifice of virgins and Athenean citizens. Cortázar, however, sides with the Minotaur, against Minos and the Athenean king, Theseus, who enters the labyrinth to slay the Minotaur. The monster's half-sister, Ariadne, who in the legend aids Theseus by providing him with a ball of string so that he can find his way back out of the labyrinth, in Cortázar's version sides with the Minotaur, and hopes he will destroy the Athenean and follow the thread out himself.

Cortázar is not simply siding with the underdog, he is stressing the importance of the unconventional: "Theseus is portrayed as the standard hero, a typical unimaginative conventional individual rushing head on, sword in hand, to kill all the exceptional or unconventional monsters in sight. The Minotaur is the poet—the being who is different from others, a free spirit, who therefore has been locked up, because he's a threat to the established order."[25] This defense of the unique in the face of the standard runs through most of Cortázar's writings, as does the theme of the labyrinth. These characteristics aside, *Los reyes* is quite different from Cortázar's later work. It is rendered in an extremely rhetorical, polished, and lofty style, as the opening passage, spoken by King Minos, indicates (the labyrinth, constructed by Daedalus, was built in the form of a snail shell): "La nave llegará cuando las sombras, calcinadas de mediodía, finjan el caracol que se repliega para considerar, húmedo y secreto, las imágenes de su ámbito en reposo. ¡Oh caracol innominable, resonante desolación de mármol, qué fosco silencio discurrirán tus entrañas sin salida!" (The ship will arrive when the shadows, calcined by midday, simulate the snail which withdraws into its shell to meditate, humid and secret, the images of its restful confines. Oh! Unnameable snail, resonant desolation of marble, what deep silence must wander through your exitless bowels!).[26]

Despite this lofty style, the work is quite readable and enjoyable, and its message is clearly expressed by the Minotaur as he confronts his attacker: "Mira, sólo hay un medio para matar los monstruos: aceptarlos" (Look, there is only one way to kill monsters: accept them [71]). Furthermore, *Los reyes* makes clear the attitude that Cortázar would always maintain toward typical, nonthinking heroes, as Theseus himself proclaims, "Los héroes odian las palabras!" (Heroes hate words! [74]).

More than twenty years later, Cortázar published another highly poetic text, *Prosa del observatorio*,[27] which stands as one of his finest nonfiction achievements. In this volume, inspired by a series of photographs of the observatories of Sultan Jai Singh in Jaipur and Delhi, India, and by an article on the migration of eels by Claude Lamotte,[28] Cortázar combined science, architecture, photography, and a sense of mysticism into beautiful, flowing poetic prose. As Martin S. Stabb observes, to appreciate this text fully, the reader must avoid searching for clearly stated facts and arguments and accept instead "the author's invitation to become enmeshed in the rhythm, in the textual flow of the piece, itself suggestive of the cosmic forces that Cortázar is attempting to apprehend":[29]

Bella es la ciencia, dulces las palabras que siguen el decurso de las angulas y nos explican su saga, bellas y dulces e hipnóticas como las terrazas plateadas de Jaipur donde un astrónomo manejó en su día un vocabulario igualmente bello y dulce para conjurar lo innominable y verterlo en pergaminos tranquilizadores, herencia para la especie, lección de escuela, barbitúrico de insomnios esenciales, y llega el día en que las angulas se han adentrado en lo más hondo de su cópula hidrográfica, espermatozoides planetarios ya en el huevo de las altas lagunas, de los estanques donde sueñan y se reposan los ríos, y los tortuosos falos de la noche vital se acalman, se acaman, las columnas negras pierden su flexible erección de avance y búsqueda, los individuos nacen a sí mismos, se separan de la serpiente común, tantean por su cuenta y riesgo los peligrosos bordes de las pozas, de la vida; empieza, sin que nadie pueda conocer

la hora, el tiempo de la anguila amarilla, la juventud de la raza en su territorio
conquistado, el agua al fin amiga ciñendo sin combate los cuerpos que reposan.
(Beautiful is science, sweet the words that follow the course of the young eels and explain to us their saga, beautiful and sweet and hypnotic as the silvered terraces of
Jaipur where an astronomer in his day managed a vocabulary equally beautiful and
sweet to conjure up the unnameable and pour it onto tranquilizing parchment, legacy for the species, school lesson, barbituate of essential insomnia, and the day arrives
when the young eels have sunk as deeply as possible into their hydrographic copula-
tion, planetary spermatozoa now in the egg of the high lagoons, of the pools where
the rivers rest and dream, and the tortuous phalli of the vital night become calm, are
beaten down, the black columns lose their flexible erections of advancement and
seeking, the individuals give birth to themselves, separate themselves from the com-
munal serpent, risk to grope their way along the dangerous edges of the pools, of life;
and there begins, no one can know when, the time of the yellow eel, the youth of the
race in its conquered territory, the water at last a friend encircling without struggle
the bodies at rest. [27–28])

This sensuality and eroticism is present in much of Cortázar's poetic
prose and in his poetry. In his final collection, *Salvo el crepúsculo* (I salvage
the twilight),[30] he brought together many of the poems he had written over
the course of his life. Some had been published elsewhere, including in his
books of miscellany. The poems center on many themes, such as love, relationships with others, and inspirational travels. They are often sensual,
occasionally playful, at times philosophical, almost always introspective.
Some are written in Italian, and one is a mixture of French, Spanish, English, and a smattering of German. There is even one sonnet in the Shake-
spearean rather than the traditional Petrarchan style. Not all is poetry;
many poems are introduced and commented upon by the author, who even
included a short chapter he had suppressed from his novel, *Libro de Manuel*
(*A Manual for Manuel*).[31]

Particularly interesting is the final section, which is comprised of poems
written in the period 1949–51, when Cortázar was torn between continuing
to live in Paris and returning to Buenos Aires permanently. "La madre"
("Mother") portrays the classic confrontation between a young man, seeking
to be himself, and a mother, who cannot reconcile what she sees with what
she had hoped for: "Delante de ti me veo en el espejo que no acepta cambios,
ni corbata nueva ni peinarse en esta forma. Lo que veo es eso que tú ves que
soy, el pedazo desprendido de tu sueño, la esperanza boca abajo y cubierta de
vómitos" (Before you, I see myself in the mirror that does not accept changes,
neither a new tie nor hair combed in this style. What I see is that which you
see that I am, a piece broken off from your dreams, hope face down and cov-

ered with vomit [323]). Another poem from this section, "El encubridor" ("The Dissimulator"), reveals what others, presumably friends and family, are saying about him and his decision to return to Paris:

> Ese que sale de su país porque tiene miedo,
> no sabe de qué, miedo del queso con ratón,
> de la cuerda entre los locos, de la espuma en la sopa.
> Entonces quiere cambiarse como una figurita,
> el pelo que antes se alambraba con gomina y espejo
> lo suelta en jopo, se abre la camisa, muda
> de costumbres, de vinos y de idioma.
> (That one who leaves his country because he is afraid,
> he knows not of what, fear of cheese with a mouse,
> of sanity among the insane, of froth on the soup.
> So he wants to change himself like a mannequin,
> his hair that he used to glue down with lotion and a mirror
> flies free like a foxtail, his shirt is unbuttoned, a change
> of ways, of wines and of language. [339])

Whether out of uncertainty about the quality of his poetry or out of playfulness, Cortázar often referred to the poems in this collection as "pameos" or "meopas" ("peoms" or "meops"), anagrams that provided the title for his previous collection, *Pameos y meopas*.[32] Also interspersed throughout the individual texts are a number of what he called "prosemas" ("prosems"), which are short, lyrical prose pieces. Although his friend José Miguel Oviedo was unduly harsh in declaring Cortázar's poems "conmovedoramente malos" (poignantly bad), a criticism that Cortázar included in *Salvo el crepúsculo* (118), it is unlikely that he will ever attain much stature as a poet.

Nor will he be long remembered as a playwright, although his two posthumously published one-act plays, "Nada a Pehuajó" (Nothing goes to Pehuajo) and "Adiós, Robinson" (Farewell, Robinson), are both highly entertaining and thought-provoking.[33] "Nada a Pehuajó" is set in a restaurant that is visited by a wide variety of transparently symbolic characters, including a judge and an American tourist. The conversation is witty and the irony biting, as Cortázar attacks the judicial system, bureaucracy, and a wide range of social ills. "Adiós, Robinson" continues in the same vein, as Defoe's Robinson Crusoe, accompanied by his now well-educated and carefully "civilized" Friday, lands by jet on the island he immortalized in his *Adventures*. Although also witty and humorous, the play makes it quite clear that Crusoe did Friday no favors, and that the island was far better off when left to the natives, even if they did occasionally eat one another.

Two additional volumes merit some comment. *Silvalandia* might best be described as a children's book for adults.[34] This volume combines texts by Julio Cortázar with plates of the art of Julio Silva, his close friend. Silva's work contains numerous whimsical creatures, portrayed in various stages of interaction, often surrounded by or perched upon equally fanciful versions of everyday objects such as a piece of furniture or a baby carriage. The colors tend toward bright blues, yellows, and oranges, and the colors, combined with the textures, suggest a Van Gogh with a sense of humor. Cortázar's texts are equally playful, assigning imaginary names to Silva's imaginary creatures, and narrating little stories to comment upon each picture.

Territorios, on the other hand, is book purely for adults.[35] Here Cortázar describes the works, and his encounter with them, of seventeen artists whom he admired, including Julio Silva. From paintings by Pierre Alechinsky to photographs by Sara Facio and Alicia D'Amico, and even a striptease by Rita Renoir, *Territorios* suggests the range of Cortázar's artistic taste. Some of the texts were published in earlier volumes. "País llamado Alechinsky" (A country called Alechinsky), "Diálogo de las formas" (Dialogue of forms)—on the imaginative statuary of Reinhoud—and "Poesía permutante" (Permutable poetry)—on the forms of Hugo Demarco—all appeared in *Ultimo round* (Last round).[36] "Reunión con un círculo rojo" ("Encounter within a Red Circle"), which deals with the painting of Jacobo Borges, comes from the story collection *Alguien que anda por allí* (*Someone Walking Around*),[37] and will be dealt with as a short story. "Un Julio habla de otro" (One Julio talks about another), on Julio Silva, and "Yo podría bailar ese sillón—dijo Isadora" ("I could dance that armchair," said Isadora), on Adolf Wölfli, a famous mental patient who produced hundreds of works of art, were both published in *Vuelta al día en ochenta mundos* (*Around the Day in Eighty Worlds*).[38]

While these texts may be read in the indicated collections, the quality of the graphics against which Cortázar's texts play is much higher in *Territorios*. In fact, *Territorios, Silvalandia,* and *Prosa del observatorio* are all beautiful editions that readers will want to explore. *Prosa del observatorio,* in particular, may offer the best of Cortázar's poetic prose. All of these works, however, as well as *Los reyes,* the collections of poetry, and the plays, come from outside the sphere of writing that one associates with Julio Cortázar, whose fame is due to his short stories, his novels, and his essayistic writings. These selections, which provide the major focus for the remainder of this study, were not always favorably received, however.

Although he had already published three major short story collections, a novel, and several other pieces, in 1961 Cortázar was still relatively unknown.[39] Enrique Anderson Imbert, a fellow Argentine, a writer, and an important critic, reacted favorably to *Los reyes*, but thought Cortázar's early stories, many of which are now considered to be among his more important, were unsuccessful and disappointing.[40] Even after his reputation began to soar in the mid-sixties, an early reviewer in the *New York Review of Books* attacked the radically experimental *Rayuela* (*Hopscotch*) as being suitable only for snobbish French audiences, and called it "monumentally boring." Even the brilliant award-winning English translation by Gregory Rabassa was panned in the *Times Literary Supplement*.[41] Similarly, Stanley Kauffman, reviewing the first collection of Cortázar's stories in English, *End of the Game and Other Stories*, thought that "The Pursuer"—now most highly regarded—was "outstandingly the worst: a juvenile and crude story,"[42] although he liked the collection as a whole. In 1970, Rodolfo A. Borello, defending *Ultimo round* against what he termed the nearly unanimous attacks launched by Argentine critics, pointed out that *Hopscotch* too once had its detractors (they had long since disappeared), and that much of the criticism was motivated by envy of Cortázar's now great success.[43]

Of course, Cortázar had his staunch supporters as well. Carlos Fuentes, like Cortázar a major figure in what has become known as the "boom" in Latin American literature, hailed *Hopscotch* as a Hispanic *Ulysses*,[44] concluding that its author, along with fellow Mexicans Octavio Paz and Luis Buñuel, represented the vanguard of Spanish America.[45] While not all critics are likely to share Fuentes's unbridled enthusiasm, Julio Cortázar was unquestionably among the five or six most important authors of the "new narrative" in Spanish America. A handful of writers, among them Jorge Luis Borges (Argentina), Alejo Carpentier (Cuba), Mario Vargas Llosa (Peru), José Donoso (Chile), Gabriel García Márquez (Colombia), and Carlos Fuentes (Mexico), brought Latin American literature to international prominence within the span of less than thirty years in a literary flowering that has not been matched in Spanish since the "Siglo de Oro" (the golden century—the seventeenth). These figures and most other contributors to the "boom," with the important exception of Borges, also were and continue to be deeply involved in politics. In many instances, politics has been as important as aesthetics in determining an author's reception in Spanish America, and Cortázar's case is as complex as any.

Julio Cortázar was involved in Argentine politics from adolescence, and his strained relationship with the Argentine government was surely responsible, at least in part, for his decision to remain in Paris. He was nonetheless keenly aware of the attacks of his critics, as well as the disapproval of his family, as his poetry from the early 1950s suggests. Voluntary exile, for any reason, has never gained a Latin American writer the admiration of his fellow citizens. Moreover, Cortázar ignored social causes as a theme in the early years, especially in his short stories, the genre that first brought him fame. Many critics insisted on reading his stories as political allegories, but Cortázar often rejected such narrow interpretations. The vast majority of his early stories, those written well into the 1960s, were of three types: fantastic, mysterious, or psychological. While these types often overlapped to a degree, realism was rare in his early work, and social realism was nonexistent.

He first revealed his talent for realistic writing in 1960, in a short story entitled "Los amigos" (The friends).[46] This is an account of three former friends who have become active either in a mob or in a political terrorist group, and one, now known as Number Three, has been ordered by Number One to kill an old friend, Number Two. He carries out his mission quickly and efficiently. Whether the characters are mobsters, government employees, or revolutionaries (by their actions it is often impossible to tell the difference in Latin America), is ambiguous, but the story suggests a new direction for Cortázar's fiction.

At about this time, Cortázar, like most Latin American intellectuals, became a strong supporter of the Cuban revolution, and began to travel with some regularity to the island. He was not particularly vocal at first, but in 1964 he published a fine short story, "Reunión" ("Meeting"),[47] in which he portrayed, from the perspective of his compatriot Che Guevara, the revolution's first days. This story is not only highly realistic, but unequivocally political.

Soon Cortázar began to speak out, especially in essays and open letters, on political issues. In 1967 he published two important essays: "Casilla del camaleón" ("The Chameleon's Station")[48] and "Carta a Roberto Fernández Retamar" (Letter to Roberto Fernández Retamar).[49] In the former, while recognizing the need to speak out against injustices, he began to advance the arguments that would gradually show him to be one of the most elegant defenders of the literary artist who, without sacrificing his social and political ideals, demands to be left alone to write aesthetically sophisticated literature. Good artists, he argued, do not need to fly the colors of their political commitment in their creative writings: "Only the weak use their literary aptitude as compensation to make them seem strong and solid and on the right side."[50] Cortázar believed that in his own case it was not necessary to fill fiction with social comment, for his readers knew where he stood, despite the chameleon quality of his prose: "my preferred colors and directions can just be made out if you look a little closer—everyone knows I live a little off to the left, on the red" ("Camaleón" 193; "Chameleon's Station" 149).

In his famous letter to the Cuban intellectual Roberto Fernández Retamar, he elaborated on his defense. He pointed out that writers living in Europe actually have a better perspective on Latin America, for they have freer access to information. He also became more aggressive in defense of his type of fiction as he insisted that local and nationalistic literary works are often not only inferior, but may be detrimental to national interests, for they tend to become xenophobic and even racist.[51] In response to the criticism he was receiving from Cubans and from strong supporters of their revolution, he reiterated his belief that socialism offered the only hope to eliminate human exploitation ("Situación del intelectual" 272).

While recognizing that a writer has both a responsibility and an obligation to the future of all humankind, and that one cannot turn one's back on others in the name of artistic freedom ("Situación del intelectual" 278–79), Cortázar believed he was fulfilling his obligation without making artistic concessions. While he might create a story from time to time that clearly reflected his social commitment, he also required the freedom to write stories that did not ("Situación del intelectual" 274–75). During the late 1960s social themes became increasingly prominent in his writings, particularly in the essays and poetry, but remained excluded from his fiction.

The most articulate, and perhaps most important statement of Cortázar's position on art and ideology was set forth in 1970 in Paris at a roundtable discussion involving, among others, the Peruvian novelist Mario Vargas Llosa. Cortázar published the text of his own contribution as *Viaje alrededor de una mesa* (Trip around a table).[52] Evidently both writers had come under strong attack by the young idealists attending the session for their failure to provide revolutionary content in their literature. In rebuttal, Cortázar raised a number of significant issues. He pointed out, for example, that what is usually meant by "revolutionary literature" is work that exhalts or educates, not creative work that breaks new artistic ground, and that leftist critics also expect, if not demand, revolutionary themes set forth in a form that is easily understood by the average reader (*Viaje* 26–27). He went on to argue that so long as an artist's ideological position has been established and is well known, no directives and no critical dogma should be allowed to curb his creative freedom (30–31).

Cortázar gave particular stress to the need to create lasting works of art: "the most serious error we could commit as revolutionaries would be to want to adjust literature or art to suit immediate needs" (32). Furthermore, he insisted, any truly creative act is revolutionary, for it advances the present state of art and works toward the future (33). In a particularly courageous line of argument, Cortázar drew a parallel between the artist and other professionals. No one, he pointed out, would argue with a doctor about medicine, yet "every adolescent who has read three novels or written two poems feels fit to pass judgment on creative literature" (43). Politicians, in particular, often have no sense of how artistic works come into being, but rather tend to view them as mere objects that the artist produces at regular intervals (44). Cortázar went on to say that his own position should be respected because it was based purely on competence, not on snobbishness or special privilege, just as the pilot who denies passengers entrance to the cabin is neither arrogant nor pretentious (45).

Cortázar proposed that if governments—and he clearly meant revolutionary, socialist governments—would but allow greater availability of quality literature rather than the usual mediocre, socially committed works that abound, the public would quickly become increasingly sophisticated and would read much more, for readers turn to literature not just for instruction, but for pleasure. To deny them readings of the highest quality is to foster mediocrity (51).

Finally, he in effect told his detractors to get lost, that he knew what he was doing:

Shout, my friend, get angry; I will keep on writing in my own way, just as the doctor keeps curing the flu or the pilot keeps flying his plane, and you or your children will see one day that true revolution in Latin America can only be born from a maximum effort on all sides, from maximum tension in all sectors, from the search for the new man from all angles. And this dialogue that a few of us insist on maintaining today despite the shouts and the vociferations of those who prefer dictating to dialogue, is the only way to show that the job of the writer, no matter how remote it may seem to be from the scene of our combat, forms a part of this dynamic search, of this investigation in the field that pertains to us and has as its final objective the advent of the new man, socialist man, at the peak of his mental and sensible capabilities. (53–54)

These positions, that the artist must be allowed to create literature according to his or her own personal vision and that governments must leave the business of literature to the truly literate, were to remain the foundation of Cortázar's pronouncements on the subject for the rest of his life. In 1969, through the journal *Marcha* in Montevideo, Cortázar and Vargas Llosa were also involved in a polemic with Oscar Collazos, a staunch and articulate defender of what might be termed the "revolutionary" position.[53] Not only did Collazos disapprove of Cortázar's public statements on art and society, he criticized his writings and even his literary taste.

In this debate, which was roughly contemporaneous with the discussion in Paris, Cortázar was more specific in his critique of social realism, which he likened to a reef that offers a constant threat to socialism: "and it seems to me that the majority of the ships of theory or pragmatism are going to continue wrecking on this reef so long as they fail to reach a consciousness *that is much more revolutionary than the revolutionaries tend to have* of the intellectual and vital mechanism that leads to literary creation" (*Revolución* 51–52, Cortázar's emphasis).

Cortázar went on to defend the revolutionary nature of many of his works, despite their lack of specifically social comment, again taking the position that literature must be revolutionary in far more than content; it must change the very nature of literature itself. Latin America had far too few such revolutionaries: "one of the most urgent of Latin American problems is that we need more than ever the Che Guevara's of language, *revolutionaries of literature rather than literati of revolution*" (76, Cortázar's emphasis).

In 1971, when Cuban poet Heberto Padilla was jailed for writing poetry that was deemed counterrevolutionary, Cortázar joined with a number of leading Latin American intellectuals in signing a letter of protest. Unlike most, however, when the debate became particularly acrimonious, he refused to turn his back on the Cuban revolution. Instead he insisted on maintaining close ties with the island while continuing to defend his positions, pointing out that he derived his view of socialism not from Moscow but from a combination of the ideas of Marx and the situation in Latin America, and that he continued to disapprove "of all postponement of human fulfillment for the sake of a hypothetical long-term consolidation of revolutionary structures."[54]

Meanwhile, Cortázar continued writing fiction in much the same vein as his earlier works. In 1973 he published *Libro de Manuel* (*A Manual for Manuel*), a novel that included dozens of accounts of political torture and injustice that he had clipped from newspapers. The novel is still highly experimental, however, and treats its young, idealistic but inflexible revolutionaries with deliberate severity: "That book was written when the guerrilla groups were in full swing. I had personally known some of the protagonists here in Paris, and I had been terrified by their dramatic and tragic sense of action, without the slightest chink to allow in even a smile, much less a ray of sun. . . . the revolution that would come from them would not be *my* revolution."[55]

When he became involved in the political turmoil in Chile in the late 1970s, he reiterated this concern: "it frightens me to have to work with some comrades who are formidable for the type of work they are doing, but oblige me to think—and I assure you it pains me to say this—what would happen if these youths were to take charge of the revolution some day."[56] In another interview he declared, "I know the pure ideologues. I have seen them. They are terrible."[57]

Also in the late 1970s, perhaps in response to some of the criticism he was receiving from his revolutionary friends, Cortázar began to write more stories in a realistic vein. Even so, throughout his life he published only nine stories that could be termed realistic in any traditional sense, and most of these are innovative and experimental to some degree. None shows the slightest inclination to sacrifice art for political statement.

Meanwhile, he continued to speak out against the treatment of intellectuals by revolutionary organizations: "the revolutionary governing bodies, all of them, without exception, manifest with varying discretion, a visible lack of confidence in the intellectuals, and in some cases, a lack of confidence that is accompanied by a good measure of disdain. They proceed at times as if the intellectual were a form of surplus."[58] In the same interview, he went on to say that officials have no business sticking their noses into literature, any more than a writer has the right to tell officials how to solve economic or social problems: "division of labor should be based on mutual respect. And often that does not happen."[59]

This outspoken attitude naturally fueled his continuing heated debate with many Cubans, but Cortázar believed that to be beneficial: "My relations with Cuba are a bit stormy, and I am content for them to be so, because I believe that socialism has to be a route that takes into account the full development of the personality. That is to say, it has to give everything I ask for in *A Manual for Manuel*, at the beginning, all intellectual, erotic, and ludic dimensions, and freedom. In Cuba that is the intention of the revolution, but revolutions are made by men, many of whom are in error when they have to lead and manage."[60]

In 1980, at a symposium dedicated to his work held at Barnard College in New York, Cortázar seemed to have mellowed very little: "the majority of writers who seem significant to me today . . . write what their invention, their fantasy, and their creative liberty move them to write, with the fullest thematic freedom, and at the same time they reveal their full historical responsibility, their solidarity with the legitimate struggles of their peoples, taking unambiguous stances before oppressive powers or reactionary politics, and defend in many ways the cause of human rights, of national sovereignty, and the dignity of peoples."[61] However, he reiterated, these political and moral stands can be made in essays, journal articles, newspapers, etc. They do not have to be incorporated into poetry, drama, or fiction. Readers who know these authors understand their political and moral positions, and do not see even their most fanciful work as literature of evasion.

The Nicaraguan revolution of 1979, which overthrew the seemingly endless dictatorship of Anastasio Somoza, rekindled Cortázar's enthusiasm, for unlike the Cubans, who had stifled creative freedom, the new Nicaraguan leaders gave it a high priority. In his final years, Cortázar made several trips to Nicaragua and lectured and published widely on the accomplishments of the Sandinistas. In fact, the proceeds from many of his final volumes were given directly to the Nicaraguan people. Just as he had created an aesthetic monument to the early days of the Cuban revolution with "Reunión," he wrote a superb story about the Sandinista's struggle, "Apocalipsis de Solentiname" ("Apocalypse at Solentiname"). Nonetheless, in his book on Nicaragua, he urged that the Sandinistas not repeat Cuba's errors of repression, especially the Castro government's repression of homosexuals.[62]

While it may be easy to ignore Cortázar's steady commitment to both ideology and aesthetic freedom during the reading and discussion of his sophisticated and complex works, such an oversight is a mistake, for he sincerely believed that the radical literary nature of his writings was the best contribution he could offer to the cause of revolution. While he thought that more highly developed countries could be reformed, he remained convinced until his death that revolution, whether through social militancy or through armed struggle, offered the only hope for countries of the Third World, where social injustices are so firmly institutionalized, usually under the forceful eye of strong, intolerant dictators. Julio Cortázar thus sought, as he himself declared, to be a Che Guevara of literature. His success is clearly evident in the revolutionary nature of most of his superb short stories, as well as in his novels. Only the near-legendary Jorge Luis Borges can begin to rival him as a creator of short stories, and his novels have earned him a reputation that places him among the most important novelists of the Latin American "boom."

Because his fiction is so unique, Cortázar was frequently called upon to address problems of literary theory from an aesthetic and a generic point of view. He explained that his perspective on reality, and hence realism, was strongly influenced by Alfred Jarry and his concept of pataphysics, in which reality does not abide in physical, observable laws, but in exceptions to such laws. That which is inexplicable in our world pertains to another, supplementary universe, which may indeed be the true world. It is this other reality that Cortázar sought to explore in many of his stories: "Almost all the short stories that I have written belong to the genre called 'fantastic' for lack of a better name, and they oppose that false realism that consists of believing that all things can be described and explained according to the philosophical and scientific optimism of the eighteenth century; that is, as part of a world ruled more or less harmoniously by a system of laws or principles, of cause and effect relationships or defined psychologies, of well-mapped geographies."[63]

Cortázar was not satisfied with Tzvetan Todorov's (*L'Introduction au fantastique*) theory of the fantastic, because it did not adequately address his own concerns. Todorov distinguishes the fantastic from the strange and from the marvelous. When an event takes place that seems to violate natural laws as we understand them, if the event is a product of illusion or of the imagination, it is simply strange. If the event is real, then reality follows laws that are unknown to us, and we are in the realm of the marvelous. The fantastic hovers between the real and the marvelous.[64] While Cortázar rejected these distinctions, he refused to offer his own definition, although he frequently explored the subject, not only in his stories but in essays and in interviews. The fantastic of H. P. Lovecraft, for example, was for him totally unsatisfactory, because he found it "completely fabricated and artificial."[65] For Cortázar the fantastic was "something very simple, that can happen in the midst of everyday reality, during this sunny midday, now, between you and I, or on the subway, while you were coming to this rendezvous."[66]

Cortázar disapproved of efforts to dismiss the fantastic occurrences in his stories as just the imagination of a character or of the narrator, or as allegory. He tried to create works in which such interpretations would be impossible, but critics persisted in making them. For many critics, the more fantastic the story, the more rigid and monoideistic the interpretations seem to become. Perhaps this insistence on interpretation as an exercise in translation (where an object or event always "means" something else) is due to Cortázar's unique blend of the real with the marvelous. He offers his readers a world quite similar to the one they inhabit, but suddenly, and often quite casually, unreal events begin to occur. The reader's perplexity is increased by a total lack of surprise and sense of resignation on the part of the characters. The real is not supplanted by the fantastic, nor the fantastic by the real, but rather the two mingle easily into a harmonious whole in which the fantastic and the real coexist.

Reducing such fusions to simple metaphoric formulae may make the job of the interpreter easier, but it also destroys the ambiguities and hence the richness of meaning that the author so carefully sought. Cortázar's text is simply replaced by another text created by the interpreter, and the aesthetic richness is lost. As Jaime Alazraki has pointed out, the variety of contradictory readings of even one story like "Casa tomada" ("House Taken Over") invalidates all such interpretations: "'House Taken Over' is a metaphor with no possible tenor, or with a multiplicity of tenors that cancel one another."[67] The key to Cortázar's stories, and the secret of their success, is their inherent ambiguity. Interpretations that impoverish or deny that ambiguity cannot but fail to come to grips with Cortázar's art.

Cortázar's stories, then, lend themselves to a rich multiplicity of readings. Their carefully structured ambiguities go hand in hand with other equally deliberate complexities. Consequently, attempts to separate them into categories have yielded results as varied as are the interpretations of individual stories. Each system, as in the case of each interpretation, offers new insights into the stories themselves with regard to structure, content, themes, perspectives, etc., but seems inadequate to describe the rich variety. Alazraki groups the stories according to the narrator: first person, third person, dialogue, and so forth. David Lagmanovich offers five basic categories deriving from the nature of the interplay between the marvelous and the real, and an additional seven-pair typology. Instances of pairs are stories based on the structure of narrating versus stories based on the structure of what is narrated, or stories in which reality seems to change versus those in which it remains constant. This particular system itself suggests the futility of such efforts.[68]

Other typologies, such as Mac Adams's tripartite grouping of the stories into 1) stories with a first-person narrator who, after establishing contact with the reader in the narrative present, returns to the past to tell his own story but never re-establishes contact with the reader; 2) stories on the theme of metempsychosis; and 3) stories in which a narrator tells of what happened to someone else,[69] make devotees of Borges long for a category of "stories written on a yellow note pad" or "stories I read on the bus last week." This is not to belittle such attempts, which have the considerable virtue of revealing threads that are common to many of the stories, but to insist upon the complexity of the works themselves, which seem to defy categorization. Once a type is sufficiently vague to embrace a substantial group, it is either incongruous with other types or so general as to be useless.[70]

Examining the stories according to the collection or collections (many have been published repeatedly) in which they were published is equally unhelpful, for there is no underlying logic to the groupings: "A book is nothing more than the moment at which an author finished a pile of stories, put them together, and sent them to be published. The separation between one book and another is false."[71] Even Cortázar's own separation of the complete stories into four groups is puzzling. The volume titles, *Ritos, Juegos, Pasajes,* and *Ahí y ahora*[72] (Rites, Games, Passages, and There and now), clearly suggest that the author felt certain stories had affinities not shared with others, but readers will find it hard to justify the placing of "Axolotl" in the volume of rites instead of the volume of games or of passages, and this is but one example from among dozens.

Here the stories will be examined in four groupings that are substantially different from those of Cortázar, and, in fact, groupings the author himself might well reject, for they are based on the degree to which the stories correspond to what most readers would accept as a sense of mundane reality. Realism is, of course, a most problematic term, and one that has produced heated debate in recent years.[73] Here it is not intended to reflect political, sociological, or economic perceptions of what is "real" but rather what is perceived to be plausible in terms of physical law. In the words of Tzvetan Todorov, "verisimilitude is the relation of the specific text to another, generalized text which is called 'common opinion'" and "we speak of a work's verisimilitude insofar as the work tries to convince us it conforms to reality and not to its own laws."[74] For reasons of practicality, Cortázar's stories are here organized according to their verisimilitude of setting, action, and character. At one extreme are the stories of the first type, those that are the most fantastic. At the other extreme are those that are almost painfully realistic. In between are the categories of the mysterious and the psychological.

Like the divisions offered by other critics and by Cortázar himself, these groupings are far from being watertight. A story such as "Las puertas del cielo" ("The Gates of Heaven"), for example, is fantastic if the apparition of Celina at the tango club after her death is viewed as concrete fact; it is plausible mystery if one believes that the woman at the club is merely someone who looks like Celina, or perhaps that Celina did not really die; and it is psychological if one decides that the woman is simply transformed into a vision of Celina by the two protagonists' imaginations. While there is no incontrovertible evidence to support any of these readings to the exclusion of the others (although there is virtually no textual evidence to suggest that Celina is still alive), to conclude that Mauro and Marcelo see someone who looks like Celina, and that their imaginations do the rest is quite plausible. Hence "Las puertas del cielo" is dealt with as a psychological story.

Verisimilitude clearly offers its own problems in our modern world of relativity and the uncertainty principle, and indeed a major source of power in Cortázar's fantastic stories is their ability to make the seemingly impossible become real. While this view of reality may be nothing more than a perceptual fallacy, ignoring as it does many of the scientific advances of the twentieth century, including the remarkable discoveries of quantum theory, it nonetheless affects the manner in which readers react to fiction. Whether or not "mancuspias" exist, or whether it is possible for a man to exchange consciousness with a salamander, as in stories by Cortázar, are not questions that affect only the bourgeoisie. Once again, "realism" here is not a politically tinged concept or a literary mode that seeks to appropriate reality; to speak of a work's realism is simply to address the question of the degree to which it corresponds to most readers' views of what is real in terms of physical law, not to the relativistic universe of quantum physics or the miraculous world of many religions.[75]

Cortázar once stated that as a child he readily believed everything he read, that attaining Coleridge's "willing suspension of disbelief" was the easiest thing in the world for him.[76] His readers, no matter how skeptical, are almost forced to suspend disbelief by the powerful economy and structural tightness of his stories, the characteristics that he himself valued most highly: "the metaphor for the perfect story is the sphere, that form in which there is no waste at all, which encloses itself totally, in which there is not the slightest variation in volume, for if there were, it would be something else, no longer a sphere."[77] The stories are so tightly composed that their rhythm becomes almost musical, and the final sentences inevitable: "There, there can be not one word, not one period, not one comma, not one sentence more. The story has to reach its conclusion inexorably just as a great jazz improvisation or a great symphony by Mozart reaches its conclusion. If it doesn't stop there, everything goes to the devil."[78]

Cortázar's theories on the ideal short story are clearly influenced by Edgar Allan Poe, whose work he translated in the early 1950s. The best stories, Cortázar believed, are deeply felt by the author, born of a particularly moving experience, and technically well written ("Aspectos del cuento" 273–74).[79] Unlike the novel, which can develop at a leisurely pace and explore a wide variety of subjects, characters, and settings, the short story must be compact, aggressive, implacable. Novels are akin to movies; short stories are more like still photography: "Photographers of the quality of a Cartier-Bresson or a Brassaï define their art as an apparent paradox: to cut out a fragment of reality, giving it determined limits, but in such a way that this fragment serves as an explosion that lays open a much wider reality, like a dynamic vision that spiritually transcends the view taken in by the camera" (Aspectos del cuento" 265). In boxing terms, he argued, the novel always wins on points; the short story must win by a knockout.

Most of Cortázar's stories do indeed win by a knockout. Almost all quickly achieve and then sustain a high level of tension, and all but a very few are expertly crafted in Cortázar's economical style. Few fail to satisfy even the most demanding reader. Their success is perhaps due in part to the fact that many were actually written in a sort of state of inspiration: "the great majority of my stories were written—I don't know how to explain it—outside of my will, above or below my reasoning sense of awareness, as if I were no more than a medium through which an outside force were passing and manifesting itself" ("Aspectos del cuento" 267). There is certainly more involved than inspiration, however, for it is clear that there was nothing in Cortázar's life that mattered more to him than mastering the craft of fiction, and that from the beginnings of his career to the very end each story was carefully and lovingly created.

The next four chapters all deal with Cortázar's short stories, with one chapter dedicated to each of the major categories outlined above: the fantastic, the mysterious, the psychological, the realistic. This grouping is far more satisfactory than taking the works in order of publication, for Cortázar wrote stories of all four types throughout his career. Nonetheless, a sense of evolution is evident when the eighty-two stories are examined together. Of the thirty discussed under the fantastic, twenty-four were published in the 1950s and 1960s, with only six from the 1970s and 1980s. Twenty-four stories are treated as plausible mysteries; only seven come from the fifties and sixties, but seventeen from the seventies and eighties. The psychological stories are the most evenly distributed, with twelve from the earlier two decades and seven from the latter, while the realistic ones again show a strong imbalance, with only two of nine coming from the fifties and sixties.

Clearly then, the fantastic stories, which many readers consider the archetypal Cortázar, come primarily from his earlier years, while the psychological and the mysterious stories are normally much more recent. It would be a mistake to give this undeniable trajectory too much importance, however, unless the actual date of composition of a story can be verified, for in the seventies and eighties Cortázar began to publish stories that he apparently had written much earlier. Some he identified, but others he clearly did not.

The next chapters, then, treat Cortázar's stories according to general type, but they also suggest a sense of evolution. The mysterious seems to have gradually replaced the purely fantastic as the author's career advanced, while the realistic became important quite late, perhaps in response to criticism about the lack of political content in his writings. Cortázar's strong interest in the psychology of his characters, however, is evident throughout his career, as would be logical, for the step from the fantastic, the mysterious, or the realistic into a world that is viewed from a purely psychological perspective, is always a small one.

Chapter Two
Short Stories: The Fantastic

Cortázar wrote for many years, polishing his craft, before he began to publish. He felt that his early works suffered from defects of structure and from a tinge of romanticism, an element that he never eliminated but learned, in his own analysis, to control.[1] His earlier published stories were also his more fantastic. While they suggest the technique he would come to master of establishing a most ordinary world that was then invaded by extraordinary events or creatures, the invading forces were too concrete and palpable to allow for the reader's "willing suspension of disbelief." Consequently, they are among those works that depart most radically from "reality" as defined in the preceding chapter.

"Estación de la mano" ("Season of the Hand"), first published in 1967[2] but written quite early in Cortázar's career, is one such story. This work deals with a mysterious hand that visits the first-person narrator. They quickly become friends, but one night the protagonist dreams the hand is in love with his own left hand and cuts it off so they can be together. When he awakens, he hides the kitchen knife. The mysterious hand, whether because its plans have been frustrated or whether hurt by the narrator's lack of trust, disappears forever. As this brief synopsis indicates, the story is hardly noteworthy, although its publication is important for scholars who are interested in Cortázar's early writings.

A second story, also first published in *Around the Day* in 1967, is equally incredible. While the author never commented upon the date of composition, the air of absolute unreality in "La caricia más profunda" ("The Most Profound Caress") supports Juan José Barrientos's conclusion that the story is an early one.[3] In this story, which will remind readers of Enrique Anderson Imbert's "El leve Pedro" (Weightless Pedro), Cortázar tells of a man who one day discovers he is slowly sinking into the ground. Eventually he disappears altogether.

What these stories share with the best of Cortázar's fantastic works is the passive acceptance by the characters of such marvelous events. The narrator of "Season of the Hand" simply accepts the hand's presence and makes friends with it, while the protagonist's girlfriend in "The Most Profound Caress" never once remarks on his transformation, although it takes several days to complete and he suffers from intense neck pains as a result of always having to look up at her. What these stories lack that is equally significant in the better stories is a strong sense of ambiguity. Both the hand and the steady sinking of the young man are rendered in unequivocable terms. The objects and events are quite specific, with no freedom allowed to the reader for interpretation, and no room allowed to find a way to accept them as possible. This type of literature seems to cry out for allegorical interpretation, but there is no apparent allegorical intent.

The same problem is evident in one of Cortázar's most studied stories, "Carta a una señorita en París" ("Letter to a Young Lady in Paris"),[4] which, like many of the other stories, is autobiographical. Cortázar lived for a time in the apartment of a friend, a young French woman, who was out of town on business. He was frequently nauseous during this period, and, as he would do so often during his career, he turned infirmity into art. The protagonist suddenly begins to vomit up an occasional tiny but live and perfectly healthy rabbit. As always in Cortázar's fantastic stories, the victim shows no surprise whatsoever. The bunnies begin to come with increasing frequency, until there are so many they have destroyed the apartment. The "letter" is left as a suicide note, explaining why the protagonist jumped from the balcony after first throwing all the rabbits to the pavement below: "No creo que les sea difícil juntar once conejitos salpicados sobre los adoquines, tal vez ni se fijen en ellos, atareados con el otro cuerpo que conviene llevarse pronto, antes de que pasen los primeros colegiales" ("I don't think it will be difficult to pick up eleven small rabbits splattered over the pavement, perhaps they won't even be noticed, people will be too occupied with the other body, it would be more proper to remove it quickly before the early students pass through on their way to school" [*Relatos* 1: 285; *Blow-up* 44]).

While many efforts have been made to interpret the vomiting of rabbits as a metaphor for something else,[5] as Jaime Alazraki has pointed out, such readings make much of the story superfluous. Cortázar provides too much detail for such rigid, symbolic interpretations: "the bunnies are not present as a metaphor but as realities in themselves: Cortázar makes them play, eat clover, chew books, destroy things; he gives them to Mrs. Molina, he hides them in the wardrobe, he wants to kill them with alcohol. The vomited bunnies are like all rabbits: nothing in their behavior—other than their fantastic origin—makes us think of an allegory. Neither are they simply an aspect of the imagination."[6]

All of Cortázar's remaining fantastic short stories differ from these three in one most important aspect: ambiguity. While the supposedly real world that is invaded by the fantastic continues to be carefully detailed, the fantastic is surrounded by a sense of imprecision, which imbues each story with a rich complex of possible meanings, none of which can be selected as correct without impoverishing the story.

"Casa tomada" ("House Taken Over") was the first story in date of publication. But because this sense of ambiguity is so prevalent in it, there is good reason to believe it was written after the three just discussed, certainly after "Season of the Hand" and "The Most Profound Caress." "House Taken Over" has suffered the fate of many of Cortázar's stories, as critics have insisted on choosing one possible metaphorical interpretation from among many, and translating the story to that single, "correct" reading. Thus it has become either a political allegory or a psychological exploration of sibling incest and condemnation of the incestuous pair by society, by ancestors, or by future generations.[7] As Alazraki points out, each of these readings is possible, but none is more correct than the others because of the story's inherent ambiguity. Any narrow reading destroys the richness of the text.

"House Taken Over" deals with a middle-aged brother and sister who live in comfort in the large home they have inherited. Their inheritance also provides an ample income, so neither works. One day the brother, who narrates, hears a noise in an adjoining room and realizes that "they" have invaded the house. He bolts the door that will seal off that portion of the building, and tells his sister what has happened:

—Tuve que cerrar la puerta del pasillo. Han tomado la parte del fondo.
Dejó caer el tejido y me miró con sus graves ojos cansados.
—¿Estás seguro?
Asentí.
—Entonces—dijo recogiendo las agujas—tendremos que vivir en este lado.
("I had to shut the door to the passage. They've taken over the back part."
She let her knitting fall and looked at me with her tired, serious eyes.
"You're sure?"
I nodded.
"In that case," she said, picking up her needles again, "we'll have to live on this side." [*Relatos* 3:10; *Blow-up* 12])

As is typical in Cortázar, neither surprise nor protest is registered: the two protagonists, unlike the reader, seem to know perfectly well who or what "they" are. The invasion continues until the couple is forced to leave the house, without even having time to get proper clothing, money, or other necessities. In a final gesture of humanitarian generosity, the brother locks the door and throws the keys down a grate in the street: "No fuese que a algún pobre diablo se le ocurriera robar y se metiera en la casa, a esa hora y con la casa tomada" ("It wouldn't do to have some poor devil decide to go in and rob the house, at that hour and with the house taken over" [12; 14]).

The dreamlike quality of this story, also evident in many others, is not incidental, for many of Cortázar's stories are based on recurring dreams, often nightmares, that he suffered. "House Taken Over" was a nightmare that came to him repeatedly. The only significant change he made in the story version was to make the displaced inhabitant of the house two persons instead of one, and to suggest subtly an incestuous relationship.[8]

Another early story, "Bestiario" ("Bestiary"),[9] falls somewhere between the ambiguity of "House Taken Over" and the discomfiting specificity of "Letter to a Young Lady in Paris." Here the intruding element is a tiger that roams, apparently at will, through a large country home. When the protagonist, Isabel, a young cousin from the city, comes to visit for the summer, she quickly adapts to the fact that the tiger may be in any room at any time. Everyone calmly accepts its presence, but all are careful to avoid the room it happens to be in at any specific time. One of the adults in the story, Nene, evidently an uncle, is particularly unpleasant to everyone, and seems, at least to Isabel, to force sexual favors from Rema, who is one of Isabel's favorites, but whose familial tie is unclear. After a particularly unpleasant series of events involving Nene, Isabel assures everyone that the tiger is in Nene's study, so that he retires to read his newspaper in the library, where the tiger actually is. After the tiger has destroyed Nene, Rema gives Isabel a hug of gratitude, as if she suspects Isabel deliberately tricked their tormentor.

As is usually the case in such stories, critics have carefully searched for metaphoric translations. The tiger has been seen as a "fantastic projection of the incestuous voracity of a family member,"[10] and in another instance Isabel's motive is attributed to her homosexual passion for Rema and her resulting jealousy of Nene.[11] The former reading assumes that Rema is not a maid, but a relative, while the latter assumes Isabel's homosexuality. While either interpretation is interesting from a speculative point of view, such speculation is not necessary to a complete reading and full appreciation of the text. As Omar Prego has pointed out, the fantastic element is not so much the presence of the tiger, but its acceptance by the humans in the story.[12] Noteworthy in "Bestiary" are Cortázar's rendering of the psychology of children, which will be evident in many of the psychological stories, and the significance of living in accordance with a set of rather arbitrary rules. Here it is Isabel's violation of the house rules (lying about the location of the tiger) that results in Nene's death. "Bestiary," significantly, is based on a delirium the author suffered during a high fever.

Partly in reaction to the critics' penchant for interpreting the fantastic events of many of his stories as the result of the main character's imagination, Cortázar made the protagonist of "La puerta condenada" (The blocked off door)[13] "the least imaginative being in the world."[14] This no-nonsense businessman, Petrone, checks into the hotel Cervantes in Montevideo (a real hotel that Cortázar himself had stayed in). Although the hotel manager has assured him that his only neighbor is a single woman, the first night he is awakened by the sound of a baby crying, a disturbance that recurs the following night. Exploring for the source of the noise, he finds a locked door sealed off by a heavy wardrobe. The following day he complains to the manager, annoyed more at having been lied to than at the noise, but once again receives assurances that there is no baby in the building. When he is again awakened, he moves the wardrobe, presses his face against the abandoned door, and echoes the wailing. A woman, whose voice he has heard each night as she tries to comfort the child, shrieks. The next morning, his female neighbor, who has been a permanent resident of the hotel, unexpectedly checks out. Nonetheless, that night the baby cries again. Petrone finally realizes that his neighbor had long lived in the company of this mysterious crying, and had tried to comfort the invisible baby so everyone could sleep. His own wailing suggested the presence of yet another child, a possibility she could not bear. As in other stories, there is no explanation for the crying child, yet it is perceived by at least two characters.

The apparition in "Silvia"[15] is much more tangible, and perceived by more individuals. The first-person narrator, who although named Fernando is clearly Julio Cortázar himself because of the names of his friends, discovers Silvia at a dinner party while playing with his friends' children. When he asks the adults about her, he is told she is just an invention of the children. He thinks they are all playing a joke on him, and takes advantage of every opportunity to observe the beautiful young woman. Eventually he learns that indeed there is no Silvia, that she is just a pretend friend of the children. He, however, has seen her on several occasions, always when the children were present. At last even they deny her existence. If the descriptions of Silvia were not so captivating and so sensual, she might be passed off as a figment of the narrator's imagination, thus making the story more psychological than fantastic. Nonetheless, the apparition seems quite real, perhaps testimony to Cortázar's always childlike imagination.

No such explanation is possible in "El ídolo de las Cícladas" ("The Idol of the Cyclades"),[16] which is quite different from the stories in which a fantastic "other" reality invades the quotidian world of the characters, for here the characters themselves are taken over by the magic spell cast by a primitive statue they have dug up on a Greek island. Somoza, an archaeologist, keeps the statuette at his summer cottage to try to replicate it, while Morand and his wife, Teresa, return to their home. Two years later, Morand gets an urgent call from Somoza, requesting him to come to the cottage. Sensing that his friend has gone mad, Morand calls Teresa and tells her to meet him at Somoza's. He arrives first. After a few minutes of conversation, Somoza begins to mutter meaningless (in Morand's world) phrases about hunts, caverns, smoke, deer, and, more important, sacrifice. He speaks of the music of flutes, and of the intense heat, as he slowly disrobes. Without warning, he attacks Morand with a stone hatchet, but in the struggle Somoza, not Morand, is killed.

As he waits for his wife, Morand soaks his hands in Somoza's blood, caresses the statue, and hides in wait behind the door: "Apoyando el hacha junto a la puerta empezó a quitarse la ropa porque hacía calor y olía a espeso, a multitud encerrada. Ya estaba desnudo cuando oyó el ruido del taxi y la voz de Thérèse dominando el sonido de las flautas; apagó la luz y con el hacha en la mano esperó detrás de la puerta, lamiendo el filo del hacha y pensando que Thérèse era la puntualidad en persona" ("Leaning the hatchet up against the door, he began to strip off his clothes, because it was getting hot and smelled stuffy, the caged herd. He was naked already when he heard the noise of the taxi pulling up and Teresa's voice dominating the sound of the flutes; he put the light out and waited, hatchet in hand, behind the door, licking the cutting edge of the hatchet lightly and thinking that Teresa was punctuality itself" [*Relatos* 1: 264; *Blow-up* 34]). Clearly this is not a case of madness, or of the inexplicable presence of a fantastic being, but an instance of possession that affects both characters. Teresa will either become a sacrifice or, if things turn out as in the previous case, she too will disrobe, take the hatchet, and go in search of another victim.

A spell of some sort also seems to be responsible for the supernatural powers of the title character in "Las fases de Severo" ("Severo's Phases"),[17] in which a family and friends gather to spend the night and observe Severo as he goes through a series of spells. The final two phases are of particular importance, for in one he gives each person a number, which appears to represent the order in which they will die, and in the other he gives each a time, possibly the time of death. The spells are familiar, for those gathered clearly know what phase is coming next, and only the last two are out of order. After Severo falls asleep and the crowd begins to disperse, a child asks the narrator, whose name happens to be Julio, if it was all just a game. Julio assures him that it was. Julio's number is two, meaning he will be the second to die. While there is nothing overtly fantastic about these particular events in "Severo," one phase is fantastic indeed. After the phases of sweating and of jumping comes the phase of moths, during which the room fills with moths that, although drawn there by gas lamps, all settle on Severo's face, creating a living mask.

"Cefalea" (Migraine)[18] also seems less fantastic than many of Cortázar's stories, except for one extremely important detail—the presence and significance of the *mancuspias*, which are nonexistent animals that combine characteristics of a variety of farm animals, including chickens and sheep. The main characters are mancuspia ranchers who live in relative isolation because townspeople are afraid of catching diseases from their animals. Of equal importance is the characters' chronic hypochondria, for they ingest a wide variety of medicines for all types of disorders, both physical and mental. Suddenly, before the mancuspias can be marketed for a nice profit, everything goes to the devil. The hired hands, Chango and Leonor, run off together, leaving the ranchers to care for the animals without help. They are unequal to the task, and the story ends with them barricaded in their house as the mancuspias, many of whom have died from inadequate care, howl around them. As is always the case with a Cortázar story, critics have found many allegorical explanations for events in "Cefalea," but perhaps the best key is offered by the title itself. Cortázar suffered throughout his life from migraine headaches; this story may be his attempt to describe one. Or if one accepts the existence of mancuspias, then perhaps the events described are not so strange, for the animals may really cause all of the mental and physical problems suffered by their owners, and perhaps it is actually fear of these diseases that keeps the townspeople away and leads Chango and Leonor to abandon the ranch. As usual in Cortázar, the story raises more questions than it answers.[19]

"Con legítimo orgullo" ("With Justifiable Pride")[20] is reminiscent of "Cefalea" in its seeming logic violated by unbelievable details. This story tells of a village in which, every fall, the townspeople gather to collect and remove the dead leaves from the streets and the cemetery. However, they do not use rakes. Instead, the elderly spray the leaves with snake essence, after which mongooses are released to gather up the leaves and place them in bags. The snake essence is gathered in the forests to the north, and since many townspeople are killed in its pursuit, the cemetery grows rapidly, necessitating the collection of more snake essence, resulting in more graves, requiring more essence. The text is accompanied by a picture of an enshrouded body and by photographs of piles of dead leaves that look uncomfortably like the skeletal remains found in mass graves. "With Justifiable Pride," although it has been largely ignored by the critics, perhaps because of its inclusion in the dazzling *Around the Day*, is an excellent story that merits careful attention. Two additional stories, both from late in the author's career, offer a mundane world that is suddenly invaded by the inexplicable. They are "Verano" ("Summer")[21] and "Anillo de Moebius" ("Moebius Strip").[22] In "Summer" a couple in a jaded relationship is asked to keep a young girl overnight. During the night a white horse, in a state of wild agitation, circles the house and appears to want to break in. The wife believes the girl has come to let the horse into the house. During the sleepless night, the husband forces himself on his terrified wife, and the couple has sexual relations, presumably for the first time in many months. The next morning, however, the husband realizes that nothing has changed, that the inevitable tired routine will now return.

Curiously, Cortázar himself has offered an interpretation for this story: "if one wants a delusional explanation, that white horse is to a degree the incarnation of the sense of guilt of the two characters who are coming to the end of their personal relationship."[23] As Rosalba Campra has pointed out, the horse in and of itself is perfectly normal, as is, perhaps, its appearance.[24] The fantastic is a result of the horse's appearance in this particular place at this particular time. However, the story could easily be read as a plausible mystery.

There can be no such uncertainty with regard to "Moebius Strip," a story in which a young British schoolteacher on a solo bicycle tour of France is raped and killed by a man she encounters in the forest. For many readers, "Moebius Strip" may be Cortázar's most troubling, most unpalatable story, not simply because of the rape, but because the young woman, Janet, enjoys it. She is killed by her attacker because of her struggles, but she is not struggling to escape, but because she wants Robert, the rapist, to use lubrication. While he is awaiting execution for his crime, Janet's spirit gradually recomposes itself and, propelled by strong sexual desire, visits him in his cell. He commits suicide, and Janet's spirit waits for his to recompose so they can consummate her passion.

Technically, "Moebius Strip" is extremely well done. The portions that describe the gathering of Janet's soul are particularly poetic, and the intercutting of the perspectives of the two main characters is most effective. Nonetheless, the theme of the young woman who takes pleasure in being raped suggests the kind of male sexual fantasy that some readers will find too common in the Cortázar of the seventies and eighties. While critics have seemed reluctant to criticize a writer of Cortázar's stature on such a point, Alicia Helda Puleo, one of the few to lament the author's sexual attitudes, is clearly correct in her description of the story: "The extraordinary formal beauty of this text invites us to forget its content, which we can sum up in the following points: a) the rapist is a victim of the society that punishes him; b) society does not understand that the soul of the slain girl is grateful, from beyond the grave, for having been awakened to sexual desire; c) the sexual desire of the dead young woman is a current that passes through their being and laboriously opens up a way through the unconscious to again find her benefactor."[25] Nonetheless, as Puleo points out, there are also a number of nonviolent sexual relationships in Cortázar's fiction, and as "Summer" attests, the victims of sexual assaults do not always find pleasure in the experience.

In terms of the fantastic, "Moebius Strip" stands somewhere between the stories in which quotidian reality is invaded by an inexplicable "other" reality, and those in which characters and events seem to slip into another time frame, perhaps even into another space. "La autopista del sur" ("The Southern Thruway"),[26] a far less ominous work than "Moebius Strip," is clearly of the latter type. A typical weekend traffic jam, created by the thousands who try to return to Paris on Sunday evening, does not begin to move again in the usual minutes or even hours. In fact days pass with the cars managing to advance no more than a few yards. Characters develop relationships with the occupants of other cars in relatively close proximity. Small societies spring up to administer the securing and sharing of food, water, and clothing. Station wagons become ambulances, and one car, whose trunk can be tightly sealed, becomes a repository for the dead. Apparently only a few days go by, but the seasons change, then change again. When at last the cars begin to move, since they progress at different speeds, the society is dissolved. The characters, despite their anger and frustration of the early days, now have difficulty accepting the fact that tomorrow they will be back at their jobs. The main character, who has fathered a child with the woman from a nearby Dauphine, will never see the child and will never see its mother again, for they did not bother to exchange names or addresses.

This story, like many of Cortázar's fantastic works, will remind many readers of the American television series "The Twilight Zone." Suddenly, on a perfectly normal day, an individual, or a group, enters another, inexplicable dimension: "It is a group of people who, in effect, enter a time dimension unthinkable for us but that for them becomes so real that seasons pass, there are loves, deaths, pregnancies, and at some moment, click, the spell breaks and everything returns to normal time."[27] One assumes that the rest of the world is immune to this temporal slippage, and that no one who was not in the traffic jam is aware of what has happened.

A similar idea lies behind the plot of "El otro cielo" ("The Other

Heaven"),[28] in which a young stockbroker living in Buenos Aires in the mid-twentieth century is able to transport himself at will to the Paris of the late nineteenth century. He is engaged to be married in Buenos Aires, but has found a lover among the prostitutes of Paris. The sights, and particularly the odors, of arcades in each city provide the necessary bridge to pass from one to the other. Apparently, neither world is aware when he is gone to the other, and both accept his presence without question. Eventually the protagonist marries his fiancée in Buenos Aires, and once married no longer visits Paris, although he often and fondly remembers the "other heaven." Although time and space now appear to be normal for all characters, including the protagonist, the reader senses that if the young man so willed it, he could again slip off to Paris at any moment.

The cogs of time also slip somewhat in "Sobremesa" (After dinner),[29] an epistolary story that begins with an invitation from Federico Moraes to Alberto Rojas for dinner with a group of old friends. The letter is dated 15 July 1958. The next letter, dated the previous day, is from Rojas to Moraes, thanking him for the excellent dinner (presumably the same one he is about to be invited to), and informing him that there seems to be difficulty between two of the other guests, both old friends of the correspondents. One has evidently been accused by the other of spying. On 16 July Moraes again writes Rojas, congratulating him on his prank and on his telepathetic powers regarding the upcoming invitation, but rebuking him for his questioning of Funes's honor. Funes and his accuser, Robirosa, as well as another guest, Barrios, have all accepted the dinner invitation. Two days later, Rojas writes Moraes expressing his own confusion at being invited back to dinner so soon, forgiving his host for defending Funes purely out of friendship, and informing Moraes he had just heard of Funes's suicide. The final letter, dated 21 July, cancels the dinner because of the death of Funes.

"Sobremesa" has not been one of Cortázar's more successful stories. Its English version is not readily accessible, and it has received minimal critical attention. It is, however, an enjoyable little story that brings to mind Jorge Luis Borges and even Macedonio Fernández.

"Las armas secretas" ("Secret Weapons"),[30] a far superior story artistically, is neither so whimsical nor so gentle. This piece is classic Cortázar in its artistic blending of two separate realities. The author himself has described the plot as one in which a phantom, killed by members of the French Resistance because he had raped a French girl, takes over the body of the young Frenchman who is in love with her.[31] This brief synopsis, or even an extended gloss running several pages, can hardly do the story justice.

In this, one of his longer stories, Cortázar develops at an almost leisurely pace the modern-day reality of four young friends: the victim, Michèle, her boyfriend, Pierre, and her friends, Babette and Roland. Michèle, after much hesitation and doubt, invites Pierre to visit the family vacation home in Pont Neuf. Pierre, however, is slowly being taken over by the young Nazi. For no apparent reason he is disturbed by thoughts of a shotgun: "Una escopeta de doble caño no tiene nada de raro, pero qué puede hacer a esa hora y en su pieza la idea de una escopeta de doble caño, y esa sensación como de extrañamiento" ("There's nothing strange about a double-barreled shotgun, but what could a double-barreled shotgun and that feeling of missing something, what could you do with it at this hour and in his room?" [*Relatos* 3: 121; *Blow-up* 223]). He remembers a German song and senses surprise that he understands it without its being translated for him. He embraces Michèle with increasing harshness; he confuses the stairway at Pont Neuf with that at the house in Enghien, where, as a Nazi, he had raped her; he becomes haunted by a vision of dry leaves: "es como si las hojas secas se levantaran y le comieran la cara en un solo y horrible mordisco negro" ("it's as if the dry leaves were coming up to meet his face and were eating it in one single horrible black bite" [129; 232]). Once at Pont Neuf, the pace of transformation increases, and Pierre becomes increasingly haunted by the German song, the stairway, the shotgun, and the dry leaves. His desire to rape Michèle increases, but he has begun to part his hair in the middle and to speak with a stutter, enabling her to recognize the German in him. She escapes and calls her friends Roland and Babette. Unfortunately, Michèle convinces herself that she is simply being haunted by her own recollections and imagination, so she welcomes Pierre back into the house where the inevitable attack takes place. As Babette and Roland approach the house, Roland tells how, seven years earlier, he had helped to execute Michèle's attacker. All of the images now flow together, the German's arrogance, his stutter, the shotgun, "cómo cayó, con la cara hecha pedazos entre las hojas secas" ("how he fell, his face blasted to bits among the dry leaves" [143; 247]).

"Secret Weapons" is clearly not only one of Cortázar's finer stories, but a masterpiece of short fiction. No analysis can possibly capture its flavor or its aesthetic perfection. Its excellence is due in large part to the degree to which it resists unambiguous interpretation.[32] As Evelyn Picon Garfield has pointed out, the collection for which it serves as the title story would have been sufficient to guarantee Cortázar's fame.[33]

In his next collection, Cortázar published another story dealing with sexual violence and temporal disjunction, "El río" (The river).[34] This piece is also set in Paris, and again deals with a married couple. The husband narrator speaks to "tú," the wife narratee, who the previous night threatened to throw herself into the river. He belittles her lack of courage and rapes her. As in other stories she begins to enjoy her violation. Suddenly the husband realizes he is making love to a corpse—that she did indeed drown herself the previous night. "El río" is an acceptable story, but far inferior to "Secret Weapons." One reason for their inequality is length: "Secret Weapons" is eight times as long as "El río," and Cortázar took full advantage of that expanded space to weave a rich tapestry of details and motifs that he then blended into a powerful ending. In "El río" the knockout comes before the spectators have taken their seats.

Another story from the quintessential Cortázar is "La noche boca arriba" ("The Night Face Up"),³⁵ which may well offer the best interpenetration of temporal realities. In 1952 Cortázar wrecked his Vespa while trying to avoid hitting an old woman who was crossing the street. He was injured badly enough to be hospitalized. The accident and convalescence provided the inspiration for this story.³⁶ The protagonist loses consciousness momentarily as a result of the impact. When he comes to, he is bombarded with sensations of pain, blood, and scraps of the remarks of onlookers and those who are trying to help him. He is carried into a nearby pharmacy to await the ambulance. His right arm is badly injured, and he apparently has suffered some internal injuries. In the hospital he is X-rayed and rushed into surgery, where, presumably under the influence of the anesthetic, his dream begins.

In his dream, which is unusual from the outset because of the odors, he is a Moltec Indian, fleeing from Aztec pursuers. When he leaps to try to escape the foul odor, he awakens to a hospital bed, suffering the thirst of a man who has run for miles. When he drifts back off to sleep, he slips back into the dream, this time to be captured. As he slides back and forth between the dream and reality, both stories move slowly forward. The patient is particularly disturbed by a temporal void that seems eternal in his recollection of the precise moment of the accident. Gradually the situations of both patient and captive become increasingly similar: the patient is on his back, in traction, which the captive is tied, spread-eagle, on his back; both have injured right arms, both are plagued by odors and by thirst.

The man discovers that he can escape from the terror of the dream by forcing himself awake, but staying awake becomes increasingly difficult. Finally, he slips back into the Aztec world, and despite his efforts to escape being sacrificed to the gods, he is unable to awaken. As he sees the priest coming forward with the stone knife poised to remove his living heart, he realizes that this is his reality, and that the dream world was "el otro, absurdo como todos los sueños; un sueño en el que había andado por extrañas avenidas de una ciudad asombrosa, con luces verdes y rojas que ardían sin llama ni humo, con un enorme insecto de metal que zumbaba bajo sus piernas" ("the other, absurd as all dreams are—a dream in which he was going through the strange avenues of an astonishing city, with green and red lights that burned without fire or smoke, on an enormous metal insect that whirred away between his legs" [*Relatos* 1: 221; *Blow-up* 66]).

"The Night Face Up" provides an excellent illustration of Cortázar's ambiguity. Critics have been divided on a number of issues concerning the story, particularly on which of the two worlds is dream and which reality. Some believe the modern world is real, others the Aztec world. Still others argue that both are equally real and that the character has simply fallen into a different time, while some see the story as an exploration of metempsychosis. Cortázar himself apparently saw it as a simple inversion; that the Indian was real, the motorscooter rider his dream.[37] However, all such single-minded readings impoverish the story, which derives its force and its richness from the equal validity of all of these possibilities. Moreover, it is unnecessary to choose whether the modern city is Mexico or Paris, although the former suggests another tantalizing possibility: that the two characters (one of whom may simply be a reincarnation of the other) occupy the same physical space, but at different times. As is often the case with Cortázar, the greatest pleasure for the reader derives from accepting all of these readings as possible; indeed, there is no conclusive evidence to suggest one is more likely than the others.

"Todos los fuegos el fuego" ("All Fires the Fire")[38] treats a similar theme with equal precision. In this case a Roman proconsul, his wife, and a gladiator become inextricably intertwined with three modern Parisians. Each story involves a love triangle of sorts. In the Roman period, the proconsul, jealous of his wife's interest in the gladiator, pits him against impossible odds. Thus Irene, the wife, is forced to watch the gladiator's death. In the modern world, Roland's indifference to his former lover's plight results in her committing suicide while talking to him on the phone. The Roman story ends in a fire that engulfs the stadium where the fight took place; the modern story ends in a fire that destroys the apartment building where Roland and his new lover, Sonia, are sleeping.

The main characters do not correspond precisely in this case. The cruel proconsul, for example, is at first paralleled by Roland, but by the end seems more akin to Sonia. The proconsul's wife and Marcos, the gladiator, both seem to flow into Jeanne, the rejected woman of the modern story. A wealth of detail, however, makes the Marcos/Jeanne tie the stronger of the two: both are seemingly helpless victims of others, both die before the fire and independently of it, the death of each is witnessed (Marcos's by the entire crowd, Jeanne's by her cat), a twitching hand is the last sign of life for both.

As in the case of "The Night Face Up" a series of motifs bind the two internal stories together. In "The Night Face Up" traffic lights become colored fires that burn without smoke, a surgeon with scalpel in hand becomes a priest with knife poised for the sacrifice, the odor of the hospital becomes the odor of the swamp. In "All Fires the Fire" the indecipherable noise of the crowd at the Roman circus becomes background noise from a bad connection between Jeanne and Roland. If "All Fires the Fire" seems less precisely balanced, it is because of the number of characters involved and their imprecise correspondence to one another. One, the gladiator, Marcos, becomes the vehicle for many of Cortázar's repeating motifs. Before the fight, for example, he dreams he is a netted fish, suffocating out of the water, and that the proconsul refuses to pay him. He understands the dream only when he discovers that his opponent is a retiarius, a man armed with net and trident. He will suffocate and not be paid because he will lose.

On the level of discourse, both stories provide precise models of Cortázar's presentational technique. At the beginning, only one world is presented, but it is offered with considerable detail. A clear, well-defined break separates this primary world and time from the second, which typically begins with a new paragraph, often after double spacing. The second reality is presented only briefly, but with enough detail for the reader to discern certain similarities between it and the original story, which, after another clear break, is developed more extensively. Gradually the embedded story occupies more and more narrational space. The extra spacing between pivotal paragraphs disappears, then stories switch in the middle of the same paragraph, then mid-sentence, then switch and switch again in the same sentence. By story's end the two worlds, the two narratives, are inextricable. In "All Fires the Fire," when the fireman states there is no hope for the inhabitants of the apartment, the reader knows there is no hope for the proconsul and Irene. The death of the Motec is also the death of the hospital patient.

"La isla a mediodía" ("The Island at Noon")[39] performs the same magic, but somewhat less effectively. In this story, an airline steward becomes fascinated by a Greek island, Xiros, that his plane passes over every midday on its flight from Rome to Teheran. He becomes so preoccupied with the island that he visits it on his vacation and decides to stay there forever, even though it is inhabited by only a handful of fishermen and their families. When the Rome–Teheran plane passes over as he strolls along the beach, he remembers how he used to peer out the window, imagining what it would be like to be on the beach below. The plane suddenly crashes into the sea, and the protagonist, Marini, is able to recover only one body—it is his own. When the fishermen come to the site of the crash, they find only the body from the plane, and apparently have no knowledge of the living Marini with whom they were visiting only the night before.

Cortázar got the idea for "The Island at Noon" during a flight from Rome to Teheran. He did not know the name of the tiny island he could see from his window, and realized that the steward would not know either. For the story, he became the steward, who would have the opportunity to fly over the island daily.[40] While this story shows the same technical control as "The Night Face Up" and "All Fires the Fire," it is less satisfying. The perfect structure has begun to lose its luster; even Cortázar became bored with how well such stories turned out.[41]

Cortázar, however, was master of still another type of fantastic plot, based on metempsychosis. His first effort to explore the transmigration of souls was "Lejana" ("The Distances"),[42] which has met with mixed critical reception. A young woman, living presumably in Buenos Aires, has occasional mental flashes concerning a woman living in Budapest. While the protagonist, Alina Reyes, lives in comfort, her double suffers from the winter's cold in coat and shoes that are worn out. Alina's preoccupation with the other woman increases to the point that when she is married, she insists on a honeymoon in Budapest, despite the fact that it is winter. There she goes out onto a bridge to meet her double, then watches in horror as she sees herself walk away; her mental flashes become permanently real. Two months later, Alina Reyes and her husband are divorced.

While critics have faulted the story for being excessively geometrical[43] and because the diary form that begins the story is violated by a third-person narrator at the end,[44] "The Distances" clearly shows Cortázar's power to make the fantastic become compellingly real through the inclusion of minute but significant details, such as the broken ice under a bridge, or snow sifting into a worn-out shoe. While one critic reads the story as a confrontation between the woman's true self and her false self,[45] for Cortázar, and for most readers, such interpretation is unnecessary: "For me the end of the story is absolutely fantastic. Since in reality the beggar woman is Alina's double, what takes place is a psychic exchange; the soul of Alina remains in the body of the beggar and the soul of the beggar takes over the body of Alina, and the one who leaves in triumph is in fact the beggar in Alina's body, and that is fairly clever."[46]

Equally clever, and even more technically controlled, is the transmigration of souls between the narrator and a Mexican salamander in "Axolotl."[47] In this story, a man living in Paris becomes obsessed with the axolotl tank at an aquarium. He peers through the glass for hours, much to the discomfort of the watchman. As in "All Fires the Fire" and other stories of similar structure, once the primary level of reality is established, a secondary reality begins to take over. This time, however, there is no defined separation—the new reality cuts into the old like a sharp knife, as the opening paragraph indicates: "Hubo un tiempo en que pensaba mucho en los axolotl. Iba a verlos al acuario del Jardin des Plantes y me quedaba horas mirándolos, observando su inmovilidad, sus oscuros movimientos. Ahora soy un axolotl" ("There was a time when I thought a great deal about the axolotls. I went to see them in the aquarium at the Jardin des Plantes and stayed for hours watching them, observing their immobility, their faint movements. Now I am an axolotl" [*Relatos* 1: 200; *Blow-up* 31]).

As the story progresses, the narrator explains how this fantastic transformation took place. After many hours and days of contemplating the axolotls with his face pressed against the glass of their tank, he comes to realize that they are conscious, thinking creatures. One day he suddenly becomes aware of seeing his own face on the other side of the glass—he is on the inside looking out. While the transmigration is only momentary at first, it eventually becomes permanent, and "he" (the man on the outside) visits with increasing infrequency. The ending of the story shows Cortázar at his best, for despite critics' attempts to turn "Axolotl" into pure metaphor,[48] he manages to make it credible by even explaining how the story came to be written: "si pienso como un hombre es sólo porque todo axolotl piensa como un hombre dentro de su imagen de piedra rosa. Me parece que de todo esto alcancé a comunicarle algo en los primeros días, cuando yo era todavía él. Y en esta soledad final, a la que él ya no vuelve, me consuela pensar que acaso va a escribir sobre nosotros, creyendo imaginar un cuento va a escribir todo esto sobre los axolotl" ("if I think like a man it's only because every axolotl thinks like a man inside his rosy stone resemblance. I believe that all this succeeded in communicating something to him in those first days, when I was still he. And in this final solitude to which he no longer comes, I console myself by thinking that perhaps he is going to write a story about us, that, believing he's making up a story, he's going to write all this about axolotls" [205; 8]).

The topic changes from transmigration to reincarnation in "Una flor amarilla" ("A Yellow Flower"),[49] a piece that, because of the narrational situation, is somewhat different, though not unique for Cortázar. A middle-aged narrator tells a narratee, a man in a bar who then serves as a bridge to the reader, the entire story. Most of Cortázar's stories have no intradiegetic (within the story) narratee, and many are not told in the first person, although the perspective is usually that of a single character, thus creating a covert first-person narrative.[50] Here the first-person narrator who communicates the story to the reader simply conveys what he has heard from another character. Only enough information is provided concerning the narrational situation—the bar, the appearance of the storyteller—to create a frame within which to embed the narrative that forms the story.

The unfortunate drunk—drunk enough to tell the truth, his listener observes—has discovered that he is the only mortal, and that his mortality is his own fault. While riding a bus he had discovered a young boy who was his exact reincarnation. They became good friends, and since the boy's life repeated his almost exactly, he was able to anticipate events in the boy's future. When a serious illness came, the man took advantage of the family's trust, he suggests, to ensure that the boy did not recover: "nadie se fija mucho si los síntomas finales coinciden del todo con el primer diagnóstico . . . ¿Por qué me mira así?" ("no one pays much attention if the final symptoms have anything at all to do with the first diagnosis . . . Why are you looking at me like that?" [*Relatos* 3: 88; *Blow-up* 51]). While his intentions, he argues, were noble, to ensure that the boy did not repeat his own life of frustration and mediocrity, he later realized, while contemplating a yellow flower, the seriousness of his deed. Each person is continued into another, but he has destroyed his reincarnation, so the line is now broken. As the world's only mortal, he is the only living being who will never see another yellow flower after his death. Now he spends every free moment riding buses, hoping to find another reincarnation of himself. He has discovered, after it is clearly too late, that he wants to be immortal after all.

Cortázar obviously felt considerable sympathy for the pathetic man. The murder, if indeed it was that, was committed to spare the child. However, it is neither the theme of immortality nor the sympathy of the author that makes "A Yellow Flower" particularly interesting in the Cortázar canon, but the manner in which the story is communicated to the reader, as a story told in a barroom. While the details of the two men drinking, one listening, the other talking, give the narrative act immediacy and realism, the fact that the storyteller is inebriated to some degree inhibits credibility, for the listener (and the reader) can simply pass it off as another tall tale told by a drunk, an option not available in any of the other fantastic stories.

Another extremely important aspect of the fantastic that Cortázar treated with great success is the fusion of mundane reality with the reality of art. His best-known, and perhaps most successful, story of this type is "Las babas del diablo" (The devil's spittle, or, as it is known in English, "Blow-up").[51] "Blow-up" is particularly difficult to explain, for the author is careful to undercut virtually every "fact" he narrates.[52] At the beginning, indeed, the narrator himself seems almost helpless when confronted with the responsibility of narrating: "Nunca se sabrá cómo hay que contar esto, si en primera persona o en segunda, usando la tercera del plural o inventando continuamente formas que no servirán de nada. Si se pudiera decir: yo vieron subir la luna, o: nos duele el fondo de los ojos, y sobre todo así: tú la mujer rubia eran las nubes que siguen corriendo delante de mis tus sus nuestros vuestros sus rostros. Qué diablos" ("It'll never be known how this has to be told, in the first person or in the second, using the third person plural or continually inventing modes that will serve for nothing. If one might say: I will see the moon rose, or: we hurt me at the back of my eyes, and especially: you the blond woman was the clouds that race before my your his our yours their faces. What the hell" [*Relatos* 3: 205; *Blow-up* 100]).

The situation improves very little, for while the narrator appears to settle on the third person, he frequently and obtrusively reverts to the first. Once the story finally begins, Roberto Michel, the protagonist, who is an amateur photographer, takes some pictures of a woman and a young man who appears to be several years her junior. The scene strikes him as unsettling, for it appears that the woman is trying to seduce the boy. Moreover, the presence of a third party—an older man sitting in a nearby automobile—increases Roberto's discomfort. After he has carefully framed and taken his pictures, he is all the more disturbed by the anger of the woman, who objects to being photographed.

Several days later, Roberto Michel develops his photographs, making a large blow-up of the one of the woman and the boy. He believes his careful scrutiny of the result confirms his suspicions of having photographed a seduction. Now, however, he begins to realize that he did not save the boy, but merely postponed the inevitable. Moreover, the boy was not being entrapped by the woman for herself, but for the waiting man. The photograph begins to move before the narrator's eyes as the scene comes to life.

This synopsis, like any summary of this story, is quite misleading, for Cortázar constantly reminds the reader that everything is made up (the frequent mention of the passing clouds and pigeons furthers this purpose), and that the narrator is particularly unreliable: "Michel es culpable de literatura, de fabricaciones irreales" (Michel is guilty of literature, of unreal fabrications [213; my translation]). All "facts" are suspect, and there is no way to determine whether the woman was seducing the boy for the man, for herself, or, in fact, not at all. The reader is bound within the perceptions, and the rich imagination, of Roberto Michel. It is equally fruitless to seek a definitive, "correct" interpretation of the ending. The photograph may indeed come to life (stranger things have happened in Cortázar's stories), Roberto may just imagine it comes to life, Roberto may have been driven insane by his obsession with the photograph, or perhaps the universe has played another Cortazarian trick, reversing the photographic process so that the photographer, not the photographed, becomes eternally immobilized, while the photographed, not the photographer, goes on its way. The point is that there is no way to tell which of these many readings is correct, and therein lies the art of this particularly excellent story. "Blow-up" is more a story about literature, a discourse about discourse, than a story about a photographer or his photograph.[53]

Cortázar fused the reality of his fiction with the visual arts on two other occasions, in "Apocalipsis de Solentiname" ("Apocalypse at Solentiname")[54] and in "Fin de etapa" (End of a stage),[55] both from late in his career. The first could also be considered a psychological story, but because of its graphic, realistic presentation seems more fantastic than psychological. The narrator, clearly Julio Cortázar himself, goes to Solentiname, Nicaragua, during the Sandinista revolution. His hosts are the Nicaraguan poets Ernesto Cardenal and José Coronel Urteche. He is fascinated by an instant camera, and wonders aloud if things might not go wrong internally and a picture of Napoleon come out (an observation that enhances the probability of the "reverse photography" interpretation of "Blow-up"). In Solentiname, the narrator takes a series of pictures with his own camera, pictures of paintings by local children and townspeople, the revenues from which are to be used to support the revolution.

Some time after his return to Paris, he has his slides developed. He sits down to run through them before Claudine, presumably his companion, returns. Instead of the paintings that had so enraptured him in Solentiname, the screen fills with horrible pictures of torture and massacre. One shows the execution of Cortázar's friend, Salvadoran poet Roque Dalton, who was involved in revolutionary activities throughout Central America until his murder in El Salvador.[56] When Claudine comes in, she asks how the slides turned out. He tells her to see for herself, while he makes her a drink. Overcome by revulsion at what he has seen, he goes to the bathroom to vomit. When he returns with Claudine's drink, she remarks on how beautiful the photographs are, and inquires about the individuals who created the paintings. The narrator wonders if she may have also seen a photograph of Napoleon.

"Apocalypse at Solentiname" is a superb story that exemplifies how Cortázar was able to incorporate the radical experiments of his early fiction—in this case "Blow-up" is particularly evident—into the more realistic and even socially-committed literature of his later years. This is not to say, however, that he dedicated himself exclusively to realistic literature toward the end of his life, as "Fin de etapa" attests. In this excellent story a young woman, Diana, who is on a motor trip without her usual male companion for reasons that are not explained, visits a village museum. The paintings it contains are all highly realistic, portraying the same room, bare but for a table and chair. The museum closes for lunch before she can see the final exhibit room, which contains but one painting. As she wanders about the village waiting for the museum to reopen, she discovers a house, apparently uninhabited, that is identical to the one portrayed in the paintings. She sits at the table to smoke a cigarette. When she finally gains access to the remaining room of the museum, she discovers that its solitary painting contains the same table as the others, but with a woman, seated and smoking a cigarette. The woman appears lifeless. Diana then returns to the house, sits at the table again, and smokes another cigarette. However, the smoke no longer moves.

Malva E. Filer has pointed out the importance of painting in the later stories of Cortázar, in which the author seems to want to paint a total, static image with words.[57] Filer believes that Diana is dead at the end of "Fin de etapa," because she is motionless. Her position, and the precedents in Cortázar's fiction for characters fusing with the art they contemplate, make it equally likely that because of her fascination with the painting, she has become a part of it. Jaime Alazraki argues that the exhibit forces Diana to recognize that she is dead spiritually, and that she therefore returns to the museum to take her rightful place in the painting.[58] As usual, it is unlikely that any of these readings is more "correct" than the others.

Events are more confusing in the much earlier "Instrucciones para John Howell" ("Instructions for John Howell"),[59] a story in which a man named Rice attends the theater. He dislikes the first act of the play, but during the first intermission he is invited backstage, where he is forced to assume the role of John Howell. He is given only minimal instructions, and must improvise the part. After a fairly successful second act, he receives instructions for the third. This time, however, he perversely does the opposite of what he has been told. In the third act, the actress who plays his wife whispers to him to not let them kill her and to please stay until the end. After act three, Rice is thrown out of the play through an offstage door but he simply re-enters through the lobby to watch the fourth and final act, during which the wife is evidently poisoned. At this point the action becomes kaleidoscopic. Rice flees the theater, but while running he encounters John Howell, who says that all of the amateur actors try to save his wife, but they cannot; the important thing is to keep running. Rice does. "Instructions for John Howell" clearly plays off the concept of the world as stage, but, as in "Blow-up," events are extremely confused. As in the other stories of this type, however, the world of art and the world of its spectators become intertwined. Once Rice is evicted from the play, just as when Roberto Michel has left the scene of the photograph, he becomes helpless to intervene and his own life is apparently in danger.

The protagonist of "Continuidad de los parques" ("Continuity of Parks")[60] fares even worse. In this, Cortázar's most compact story, a man seated in a high-backed, green-velvet armchair reads about how a woman and her lover plan and carry out a murder. The house, the grounds, the stealthy approach of the killer—all are minutely described. Everything goes precisely according to the lovers' plan, right down to the final approach: "La puerta del salón, y entonces el puñal en la mano, la luz de los ventanales, el alto respaldo de un sillón de terciopelo verde, la cabeza del hombre en el sillón leyendo una novela" ("The door of the salon, and then, the knife in hand, the light from the great windows, the high back of an armchair covered in green velvet, the head of the man in the chair reading a novel" [*Relatos* 2: 8; *Blow-up* 56]). The reader, normally after a furtive look over his or her own shoulder, remembers that in the first lines the victim had signed a power of attorney and had discussed joint ownership with the manager of the estate.

Critical opinion has been divided on this account of a man who is murdered while reading a novel about a man who is murdered while reading a novel about a man . . . ; some have found it overly contrived, and others consider it brilliant. Cortázar, who almost never reworked his stories, rewrote it some fifteen times and still remained dissatisfied with the result. For him, the keys were rhythm and tension: "the rhythm builds up, accelerates, becomes more and more anguishing, like in certain nightmares, and is only relieved at the very end."[61]

"Historias que me cuento" ("Stories I Tell Myself")[62] combines the technique of embedding one story within another with that of fusing art with reality. In this case, the narrator likes to tell himself stories at night. In a favorite scenario he is a truck driver who, while traveling a remote country road at night, picks up a woman in distress. They spend the night making love in his sleeper cab. Gradually, as the story is repeated in his mind, Delia, the wife of a friend, becomes the woman in the story. After the real Delia returns from a trip to care for her mother, she tells the narrator and his wife how her car broke down one night on a remote country road and how a friendly truck driver gave her a ride. When she is alone with the narrator, she admits to him that she and the driver made love. The narrator hopes to make love to her again, as in her reality and his story, but she does not recognize him as the truck driver.

The interpenetration of realities is adeptly handled in "Stories I Tell Myself," and both the story the narrator tells himself and the version of the same episode narrated by Delia play against the backdrop of an even more real, or at least more mundane, reality in which Delia changes her baby's soiled diaper.

"Stories I Tell Myself," "Apocalypse at Solentiname," and "Fin de etapa" reveal the degree to which Cortázar, always the master of the short story, particularly of the fantastic, maintained his narrative powers until the end of his career. They also illustrate the degree to which his stories evolved away from the incredibly fantastic stories of his early years into plots that seem to be somewhat more leisurely, less contrived, and at times less trying for the reader's "willing suspension of disbelief." While "Fin de etapa" maintains the highly fantastic line of "Axolotl," "The Distances," and "Secret Weapons," "Stories I Tell Myself" and "Apocalypse at Solentiname" suggest the direction most of Cortázar's later stories took, away from the fantastic and into more plausible mysteries or into stories with psychological explanations.

Chapter Three
Short Stories:
The Mysterious

Although the fantastic dominated Cortázar's short stories from the forties through the sixties, even his first collection, *Bestiario*, contained at least one plausible mystery, and five other stories, spanning the period from 1951 to 1980, hover on the border between the two types.

"Circe" is a case in point.[1] A young man, Mario, courts a neighborhood girl, Delia, whose first two fiancés have died suddenly and mysteriously. Delia begins to create fancy bonbons of delicate flavor and crunchy texture for him, treats that he must sample with his eyes closed. Shortly after the engagement is announced, Mario begins to receive anonymous warnings and also notices that Delia always knows when an animal will die. One night, after Delia has announced the impending death of the family cat, Mario goes to the kitchen to get himself a drink of water. There he finds the cat, dying, with wooden splinters driven into its eyes. Rather than eat his bonbon for the evening, Mario breaks it open to discover it is stuffed with dead cockroaches. Presumably, this discovery saves his life.

As in the better fantastic stories, "Circe" is filled with a wealth of details that hint at the denouement without revealing it. Delia's family, for example, always refuses to sample the new candies, and even when they eat an old standard they cut it in half before tasting it. In addition, Mario has glimpsed hordes of cockroaches in the kitchen, which is quite in contrast to his mother's, where insects are diligently poisoned.

As one might expect, "Circe" was born of one of Cortázar's temporary neuroses. While he was attending translator school, a normal three-year program that he completed in only six months, Cortázar developed an irrational fear that there were insects in his food. He could eat nothing without a preliminary careful examination. During that period he learned of a pretty young woman living in Buenos Aires who was believed to be a witch because two of her suitors had committed suicide. He combined these two elements into his story, and found that he was cured of his neurosis.[2]

While "Circe" has high shock value and is therefore an unforgettable

45

story, it suffers from a number of aesthetic weaknesses, the most significant of which is the narrator. The story is told by a man who was twelve years old and living in the neighborhood at the time the events took place. Although Jaime Alazraki has argued that the choice of such a third-party, unreliable narrator is important to the success of the story, reasoning that if the narrator could explain the events the story would fail,[3] in this instance the choice is inconsistent with the details provided. The boy does not simply sketch in the major events, but offers details about the inside of the house, personal conversations, the taste and texture of the bonbons, and other minutiae that he could not possibly know. If Cortázar had intended to imply that Mario told the story to the boy later on, then he surely would have provided that detail to bridge the gap in plausibility. Indeed, if such were his intentions, he could have dispensed with the third-party narrator altogether.

Despite this flaw, "Circe" is a significant story for a number of reasons. It shows, in the first place, that Cortázar was interested not only in the purely fantastic in his early years, but that he was also concerned with the plausible but strange, something of a halfway house between harsh reality and the totally unreal events of many of his works. Moreover, "Circe" is significant in its portrayal of Delia, the beautiful woman who attracts young men with the intent to destroy them.[4]

Five years later, Cortázar published another borderline story, "La banda" (The band),[5] for which there is a perfectly logical explanation, but which could just as easily have been written as a fantastic story. In this case, the protagonist, Lucio Medina, has related the events to the narrator, thus avoiding the awkward narrational situation that exists in "Circe." One day Lucio went into a theater in Buenos Aires to view a film made by a director he particularly admired. He quickly noticed that the audience, comprised as it was of portly domestic women and working men, was quite strange for such a film. The movie was preceded by an unannounced concert, offered by the "Alpargatas" (Sandals) band, a group made up of employees of the Alpargatas Company (a real company) and their families. In fact, the band was a sham, for only about a third of the members actually played their instruments, while the majority simply pretended. The strange audience was composed of the band members' families and friends. While Lucio realized, at least intellectually, that the theater had not announced the concert because it was afraid of losing patrons who wished only to see the film, the unreality of the event pursued him long afterwards: "De pronto le pareció entender aquello en términos que lo excedían infinitamente. Sintió como si le hubiera sido dado ver al fin la realidad. Un momento de la realidad, que le había parecido falsa porque era la verdadera, la que ahora ya no estaba viendo. Lo que acababa de presenciar era lo cierto, es decir lo falso" (Suddenly it seemed to him he understood that [the event] in terms that exceeded it infinitely. He felt as if he had been allowed to see reality at last. A moment of reality, which had seemed false to him because it was the true reality, that which he was seeing no longer. What he had just witnessed was true, that is, false [*Relatos* 3: 103]). He concluded that he had been returned to his own reality only by luck. At the end, the narrator returns to point out that what happened to Lucio was not imaginary or false, that the band did indeed play in that theater on that day.

It is easy to imagine a story by Cortázar in which the mysterious events of a concert continue to dominate long after the orchestra finishes playing, and, in fact, that sort of slippage into another level of reality is the key to many of the author's fantastic stories. In "La banda," however, not only is Lucio spared, perhaps through luck, but a third-party narrator vouches for the veracity of his account. "La banda" is based on an actual experience that Cortázar had when he attended a movie in Buenos Aires, and all of the major details are, he insisted, true. Jaime Alazraki has pointed out that the "alpargatas" were supporters of Perón, whose rallying cry was "alpargatas sí, libros no" (sandals yes, books no). Moreover, the Perón government once obliged all theaters to offer a "número vivo" (live performance) before each film, to give unemployed actors and artists a chance to perform.[6] While some critics have seen the story as a veiled critique of Peronism, Cortázar rejected that interpretation.[7]

"No se culpe a nadie" (No one should be blamed)[8] departs from an equally mundane event, but turns it lethal, still without departing from plausibility. The initial situation is innocuous enough: a man decides to put on his pullover sweater before he goes out to meet his wife. Unfortunately, the material in his shirt clings to the wool of the tight sweater, leading to a titanic struggle, the details of which are familiar to all who have found themselves in a similar situation. His arms get caught in the sleeves, his face is stuck against the dense wool, which then becomes humid and sticky from his breath. He can neither proceed nor retreat. One hand seems to obey his wishes, while the other seems independent and hostile. Finally, with a mighty and flesh-scraping effort, he forces his face into fresh air, only to see, silhouetted against the dim light, his disobedient hand, fingers poised to strike at his eyes. In fright he withdraws back into the safety of the sweater, but as he runs to escape he falls through an open window, twelve stories above the street.

While "No se culpe" may not be Cortázar's finest story, few who have read it will put on a pullover without recalling the fate of its protagonist. Some may even close the window before dressing. The story is masterfully told, with a wealth of sensual detail conveying the struggle with the sweater. The deadly open window is mentioned only casually, when the man observes to himself that he must be careful not to get too near until his face is free from the wool. While the events are unlikely, Cortázar has simply taken a mundane act and carried it to an illogical but possible conclusion.

Another borderline work is "Reunión con un círculo rojo" ("Encounter Within a Red Circle"),[9] a story in which a man, attempting to save a stranger, entraps himself. The protagonist, Jacobo, enters a restaurant one rainy day, and almost immediately perceives an aura of strangeness about the place and those who work there. When a woman, an English tourist, comes in, he realizes that she is in danger from the restaurant's employees. Rather than finish his meal, he dawdles to make sure she leaves safely. He follows her out to insure her escape, then a few minutes later returns, only to discover that *he* was the intended victim and that she was the bait.

Whether "Encounter" is a fantastic story or a mystery is difficult to decide. The implication is that the woman, and the others present, are possessed, or perhaps even vampires, for now Jacobo is to join them. Like "La banda," this story is based on a real event from Cortázar's life: he entered the restaurant, sensed something amiss, and feared that all present were vampires (which he always swore he believed in). When the tourist came in, he felt obligated to protect her. Only the ending was invented for the story.[10] The story, however, does not specify that vampirism is involved, so the reader is free to imagine other possibilities, including less fantastic ones.

"Encounter" is masterfully told by a narrator who addresses Jacobo as "usted," the formal "you" in Spanish. In other words, the protagonist is actually the narratee, who listens to his own story. The narrator turns out to be none other than the woman he sought to rescue! The dedication suggests another Argentine master of the fantastic, Borges, but the Borges Cortázar had in mind was not Jorge Luis, but Jacobo, the Venezuelan painter. In fact, this story is the text that accompanies the painter's work in Cortázar's *Territorios*. In an almost labyrinthine twist, then, the author has taken an event from his own life, ascribed it to the man to whom the story is dedicated, and made the dedicatee and protagonist the narratee of the whole history. The fictional text is then used to accompany the visual texts created by the protagonist/ victim/narratee. Once readers have deciphered all of these twists and turns, they may no longer care whether the story is fantastic or mysterious. In either case it is most enjoyable.

The final borderline story, "Orientación de los gatos" ("Orientation of Cats"),[11] also fuses fiction with visual art, but in a much more obvious way. The narrator of this first-person story tells of the close relationship that exists between himself, his wife, and his cat. While he recognizes that his wife loves him unquestioningly, he has reservations, and senses that she never bares her true self. Only through observing her as she experiences art or music can he get a glimpse of the true Alana. One day, Alana is particularly enthralled by an art exhibit, and the narrator feels he is particularly close to possessing her essence. The final painting she observes is of a cat, identical to their own, looking out a window. Alana joins the cat in looking out the window, seeing something that the narrator is never able to share.

"Orientation of Cats" has much in common with the fantastic "Fin de etapa," but with an important difference. In "Fin de etapa" the woman fuses with the art and becomes an element in the painting. In "Orientation" Alana apparently remains in the world of her husband, separated from him not by the barrier that exists between art and reality but by a mysterious inner quality that she shares with the cat and that the narrator can never penetrate. The story does not clarify what that quality is, although it suggests that Alana and Osiris, the family cat, enjoy a sense of freedom, reflected in the manner in which they observe things. Further, "Orientation" suggests that the narrator wishes to possess not only the quality, but his wife and his cat as well, a wish that remains frustrated. The wife, the cat, and the cat gazing out the window in the painting all invite reader interpretation on relationships among living beings and on the role of art in our world.

Cortázar's fascination with the relationship between art and reality is evident throughout his career, and many of his mysterious stories explore the manner in which they influence one another. "Queremos tanto a Glenda" ("We Love Glenda So Much")[12] describes the manner in which the fans of actress Glenda Garson affect not only her films, but eventually her life. What is particularly unusual in this story is that the group, composed of only twenty or thirty fans, does not influence films in production, but those already finished and widely known. At first the group simply gets together unofficially to discuss whatever film they have just seen. After some time, however, it becomes clear to all the fans that many of her films suffer from slight flaws— none of which are attributable to Glenda Garson, of course. Taking advantage of the wealth of one member of the group, and through a great deal of effort, they manage to steal every existing copy of each film for retouching in their laboratory. At first they make only minor changes, but eventually they go so far as to create new endings that they find more satisfactory. Garson's retirement seems to insure, for a time, their total success, but, unfortunately for their plans, she decides to return to the screen. The group is appalled at her rash decision, but to protect her from any flawed films they decide to do the only proper thing: "Queríamos tanto a Glenda que le ofreceríamos una última perfección inviolable. En la altura intangible donde la habíamos exaltado, la preservaríamos de la caída, sus fieles podrían seguir adorándola sin mengua; no se baja vivo de una cruz" ("We loved Glenda so much that we would offer her one last inviolable perfection. On the untouchable heights to which we had raised her in exaltation, we would save her from the fall, her faithful could go on adoring her without any decrease; one does not come down from a cross alive" [*Relatos* 1: 306; *We Love Glenda* 16]).

Two years after "We Love Glenda So Much" Cortázar published an epilogue in the form of an open letter to actress Glenda Jackson, "Botella al mar" (Bottle cast into the sea).[13] The letter was actually written in 1980, shortly before the publication of *Queremos tanto a Glenda*. While the short-story collection was in the final stages of production, Cortázar and a group of his students in Berkeley went to see Glenda Jackson's film, *Hopscotch*. The coincidences, that Jackson, who is the actress Cortázar had in mind when he wrote his story, should act in a film named "Hopscotch," which is also the title of a novel written by Cortázar as well as that of a book written by the main character in the film; that Cortázar should kill the film actress in his story at the same time that Glenda Jackson was involved in the destruction of the author of *Hopscotch* in her film; that the film in which Jackson starred, like the films the characters in the story feared were to come, was vastly inferior to her finest work, were too much to resist. Cortázar's open letter, launched toward London as if it were placed in a bottle and cast into the sea, notifies Jackson of the mysterious bond between them.

Radio theater, rather than film, brings together the two main characters in "Cambio de luces" ("A Change of Light").[14] The narrator/protagonist is a famous radio actor who always plays the role of the heavy. One day he receives a fan letter, which is unusual because of the parts he usually takes. When he answers, he receives an invitation to meet the woman who wrote it. Luciana is quite different from what he imagined; she is taller, older, and most importantly has black hair and brown eyes rather than the chestnut hair and blue eyes he expected. She, on the other hand, imagined him taller, with curly hair and grey eyes. The two quickly become lovers, and then he begins to try to transform her into the vision he originally imagined. He persuades her to bleach her hair slightly, and to wear it pulled back. He decorates the apartment to match the setting in which he visualized her before they met, even though she argues that the new furniture does not match the decor. He is frequently on the verge of explaining his demands to her, but always postpones explanation. One afternoon, however, he sees her coming out of a hotel on the arm of a man who is taller than he, and with curly hair.

"A Change of Light" is a good story that deals with a theme that is often found in Cortázar's fiction: the manner in which individuals endeavor to possess and remake others. The mystery, in this case, stems from the narrator's ignorance not only of his own destructive efforts, but from the apparent insensitivity that blinds him to Luciana's pursuit of her own illusions.

This quietly simmering domestic discontent is quite in contrast to the explosive situation upon which "Clone" is based, again against a background of art with which mundane reality threatens to coalesce.[15] A group of tango artists is about to dissolve when the director, Sandro, begins to have an affair with Franca, who, along with her husband, Mario, also belongs to the troupe. A background for this intrigue is provided by the life of Carlo Gesualdo, the composer of a number of madrigals performed by the troupe, and a man who murdered his wife and her lover. As the troupe continues to deteriorate it becomes clear to all that Mario is quite aware of the affair between the director and his wife. On the afternoon of the day in which the group is to open in Buenos Aires, Mario and Franca leave to do some shopping. She never returns.

Technically "Clone" is far more significant than this rather ordinary plot suggests. In a note that Cortázar hyperbolically confesses is as long as the story, he explains the piece's composition. The structure is based on Johann Sebastian Bach's "A Musical Offering," following the instrumentation arranged by Millicent Silver. Each character corresponds to an instrument: Mario, a bass in the troupe, plays the bassoon; Lucho, a tenor, the violin; Franca, a soprano, the oboe. There are eight characters, eight parts in the troupe, and eight musical instruments. The characters (instruments) blend in each movement according to Silver's arrangement. "Clone" is a fine story even without this technical virtuosity; with it, the story emerges as a superb blend of music and fiction, perhaps the most successful such effort most readers will have encountered. The note should be considered as a part of the story itself, not only because it provides valuable insight into how the author worked, but because of the perspective it offers on the story's structure.

Many of Cortázar's other mystery stories, as might be expected, also deal with danger and murder. "El móvil" (The motive)[16] tells the story of a man whose friend is murdered over a woman. He and his friends decide to take justice into their own hands. They determine that the killer is from Buenos Aires, a sailor, and a passenger on a ship sailing for France. The narrator, equipped with a forged passport, embarks on the same ship, but is unable to identify the man he is after since the only clue he has is a tattoo and the other passengers never bare their arms. When the boat reaches France he simply kills the most likely suspect, only to discover that he has no tattoo. He then makes a secret pact with his intended victim, who helps him escape detection until he can return to Buenos Aires. The original killer thus goes free.

The plot is somewhat thickened by another story of macho honor that evolves on the ship. The narrator uses a woman he himself has been involved with to try to uncover the identity of the man he seeks. She is supposed to seduce his suspect to see if he has the identifying tattoo. However, she becomes involved with the suspect, so the narrator cannot be sure if her report of no tattoo is accurate, and the reader, cast into the role of a drinking companion to the narrator, cannot be certain if the final murder was committed as vengeance for the death of a friend or retribution for the theft of a woman.

"Relato con un fondo de agua" (Story with a background of water)[17] is much more ominous, for it places the reader in the perspective of the narratee, Mauricio, who is in danger of being murdered by the narrator. The narrator tells simultaneous tales, one of a recurring nightmare he used to suffer, and another of how he previously told the dream to Lucio, under circumstances identical to those under which he now tells it to Mauricio. In the nightmare, the narrator walked to a remote corner of the swampy island on which he now resides and found a body floating in the water. The disturbing aspect of the dream was its minute detail. After he told the dream to Lucio, the two went for a walk, which led them to the exact place where the body was found in the dream. This time, however, the narrator discovered that the body in the dream was his own, and that Lucio intended to kill him. He struck first, evidently drowning his friend. Now he is retelling the story to Mauricio, under identical circumstances: seated on the veranda on a warm night as the moon rises slowly. Mauricio is even seated in the same chair in which Lucio sat on the night of his death.

The precise relationship between dream and reality is unclear in "Relato con un fondo de agua," as is often the case with Cortázar's stories. Ana Hernández del Castillo believes that the murder actually took place before the nightmares began, and that the narrator suffers the threatening nightmare out of guilt for having killed Lucio. Cortázar never clarified the interpretation, although he pointed out the somewhat veiled homosexual relationship between Lucio and his killer,[18] a relationship that clearly had soured, thus providing motives for both Lucio and the narrator.

Another of Cortázar's more frightening stories is "Cuello de gatito negro" ("Throat of a Black Kitten").[19] This story begins casually and realistically enough: a man, Lucho, enjoys "accidentally" touching the hands of women on the subway. One day a woman's gloved hand deliberately touches his, not once but twice. Lucho strikes up a conversation with the hand's owner, Dina, who explains to him that her fingers act independently of her will, and that he should not get the wrong idea, as so many other men have done. Despite her warning, Lucho accompanies Dina to her apartment, and the two, almost inevitably, make love. After some time Dina begins to become more and more strange. Through a series of seeming mishaps they find themselves without light, and she cannot strike a match because her hands again refuse to obey. She grasps his genitals in a painful grip, and the lovers begin a violent struggle. Eventually Lucho breaks free, escaping through the door onto the frigid stairwell landing. Dina locks the door behind him. At the close of the story, Lucho huddles naked on the landing (it is the dead of winter), calling to Dina to let him have his clothes, until the police come to take him away. As Rosalba Campra has pointed out, the story is frightening because the author offers no explanation for events. Even the most monstrous would be reassuring, but none is offered, not because Cortázar is withholding information, but simply because there is no explanation for what transpired, as is the case in so many of Cortázar's texts.[20]

"Tango de vuelta" ("Return Trip Tango"),[21] though more deadly, is less threatening because it involves circumstances the reader is unlikely to encounter, since here the heroine's downfall is a direct result of her own deceit. Matilde, although married to Emilio, fell in love with Germán. To escape from her unhappy marriage, she simply ran away to Germán, telling him her husband had died. Things go well for several years for Matilde, who now has a son, until one day she sees Emilio waiting outside the house. Several days of terror ensue as Emilio takes advantage of one of Germán's business trips to make friends with Matilde's son. He eventually seduces the maid, thus gaining entrance to the house at night. Matilde, after overdosing on sleeping pills and alcohol, manages to kill Emilio when he finally attacks her, but she herself dies from her overdose only two hours later.

"Return Trip Tango" offers a number of problems that one expects to find only in early stories by Cortázar. The most significant is the matter of narrative perspective, for the story is narrated by the ambulance attendant, who could not possibly have access to the details provided in the story, even when one takes into account his claim that the maid, Flora, provided him with the information. However, the narrator is extremely self-conscious at the beginning, and confesses that not only does he love to write, he loves to embellish reality as well. This echo of Roberto Michel in "Las babas del diablo" ("Blow-up") highlights the fact that, in some ways, this story almost seems a coda to much of Cortázar's short fiction because it repeats so many of his successful themes and concepts. Matilde, for example, is reading a novel whose action parallels that of her own story, as in "Continuidad de los parques" ("Continuity of Parks"). The sleeping pills recall the death of Jeanne in "Todos los fuegos el fuego" ("All Fires the Fire"); the Malayan knife recalls that of the Indian in "La noche boca arriba" ("The Night Face Up"); and the glass ball recalls that of Michèle in "Las armas secretas" ("Secret Weapons").

"Diario para un cuento" (Notebook for a story)[22] offers no such problems of plausibility, although like "Blow-up" it begins with a lengthy series of hesitations, false starts, and self-reflexive interrogations that serve to establish the reality of Cortázar, professional translator and man of letters. In an interview, Cortázar pointed out that the story was indeed highly autobiographical. In his early days as a public translator he "inherited" his partner's business of translating letters for local prostitutes. While working on one such letter, he discovered that a woman had been poisoned. He never inquired into the matter, but for the story he let his imagination provide the details.[23]

Once Cortázar has clearly established that he himself is the narrator, through allusions to Bioy Casares and his own work as translator of technical manuals and a certain essay on Derrida, he begins the story of Anabel, who, he discovers through translating her correspondence, wants her boyfriend to get poison for her friend Marucha to use on a rival, Dolly. The narrator tries to prevent the murder without getting too directly involved, but one day reads about it in the paper. As Alazraki argues, "Diario para un cuento" is less about Anabel than about the narrator's relationship to the events.[24] The story is told in diary form, as if it were simply the notebook for the story, but as Cortázar pointed out, it is a very carefully thought-out story.[25] The journal form, the allusions to Cortázar's own reality, and the plausibility of the events narrated make "Diario" one of Cortázar's more believable mysteries.

An equal as a carefully thought-out story is "Los pasos en las huellas" ("Footsteps in the Footprints"),[26] which is perhaps the author's most Borgesian piece. "Footsteps" is a sort of detective story, which tells of a minor literary scholar who decides to write a study of a significant but obscure Argentine poet, Claudio Romero. The literary detective, Jorge Fraga, collects data for two years before writing a biography that makes both him and his subject famous. A key episode from Romero's life, discovered by Fraga, was his act of sacrificing himself and his love for Susana because he, at the time gravely ill, did not want her to endure the burden of caring for him. Some time later, now well recovered, he wrote a few poems to the wealthy Irene Paz, but he could not aspire to her or her social circles. He died shortly thereafter.

After the smashing success of his *Vida de un poeta argentino* (*Life of an Argentine poet*), and almost on the eve of receiving the National Prize for his study, Fraga discovers that the Susana/Irene episode was untrue; that in fact Romero had cruelly abandoned Susana, and indeed forced her into a life of prostitution. In his acceptance speech for the National Prize, Fraga reveals the truth to a scandalized audience. Later, he reflects that he can still have it either way: he can let the truth stand, and retire from the spotlight to his former life of quiet, responsible study, or he can, through a few interviews, take advantage of the furor caused by his speech—the cancellation of the prize and the withdrawal of a government offer of a post in Europe—to vault himself into even greater fame. Cortázar withholds Fraga's decision from the reader.

One cannot but wonder if Cortázar may not have had his tongue well into his cheek when he wrote "Footsteps," for it chronicles the tendency of literary scholars to lose themselves totally in their subjects, practically becoming one with the writers they analyse. More importantly, the story suggests the need many critics feel to discover, or even invent, major literary figures to insure their own places in history. Fraga's intellectual blindness is the result of his subconscious refusal to see any flaws in his subject. He was misled by his own eagerness to discover a literary hero: "No quise darme cuenta, no quise mostrar la verdad porque entonces . . . Romero no hubiera sido el personaje que me hacía falta como le había hecho falta a él para armar la leyenda, para . . ." ("I didn't want to see it, I refused to show the truth because, then . . . Romero wouldn't have been the famous person who needed me as I needed him to put together the legend, in order to . . ." [*Relatos* 2: 51; *We Love Glenda* 295]). The responsible, though no less competent, Fraga who worked quietly at his scholarship was both as obscure and as significant as the poet he discovered.

While many of Cortázar's mystery stories involve an element of idiosyncratic gamesmanship—the protagonist of "Throat of a Black Kitten," for example, entertains himself with "inadvertant" hand-touching on public transportation systems, and Cortázar himself wrote "Clone" according to a strict preconceived musical plan—two of the stories carry the concept of "lo lúdico" (the ludic) to its logical conclusion. Characters establish the rules of the game, then play to the end, which is death in both instances.

"Manuscrito hallado en un bolsillo" ("Manuscript Found in a Pocket")[27] is a perfect illustration of Cortázar's concept of the ludic. The protagonist/ narrator of this story devises an elaborate set of rules he must follow to meet a woman: he has to see her reflection in the window of the subway and smile at the reflection; she must observe the smile, and then follow the exact route he has determined beforehand, making connections and/or exiting the subway according to his plan. If all of this should occur, then he may speak to her. Naturally, the game has always ended before he has had the opportunity to speak. One day, however, the protagonist is particularly taken by a young woman, and violates the rules, speaking to her despite a variance in their itineraries. After several weeks of a slowly-growing friendship, he explains to her the game, the rules, and his transgression. They agree to play again. She takes a two-week vacation to dedicate to riding the subway while he looks for her according to the rules. Shortly before the two weeks run out, he sees her. The smile is given and observed. The story ends just as they are coming to the last station on the line; he now has a fifty-fifty chance of getting to speak to her, depending on her final choice. If he loses, they have agreed they will never see each other again.

The ending is hardly indeterminate, for the title explains that the story is a manuscript found in someone's pocket, and the narrator calls attention to its composition in the beginning: "Ahora que lo escribo, para otros podría haber sido la ruleta o el hipódromo" ("Now that I'm writing this, it might seem like roulette or the racetrack to others" [*Relatos* 1: 74; *We Love Glenda* 249]). Cortázar himself pointed out that the man's guilt at having broken the rules was so great that he could not do other than replay the game, following it to the end. He loses, not only the game but the woman, and, the author believed, probably committed suicide, throwing himself in front of an oncoming train.[28]

The rules are almost as strict, and the results certainly as fatal, in "Vientos alisios" ("Trade Winds").[29] Vera and Mauricio, who have been married for some time and are bored with life, devise a plan for their vacation. They catch separate planes to Nairobi, register at the Trade Winds, a spa, and, in effect, take separate vacations at the same resort. Each quickly finds a lover, and each thoroughly enjoys the vacation, with only limited outbursts of jealousy. Once the rules of the game have been satisfied and the vacation concluded, there is no reason to continue to play, so they make the return flight as a couple, but each now pretends to be the other's lover from the Trade Winds. Mauricio thus becomes Sandro, while Vera becomes Anna. Anna (Vera) invites Sandro (Mauricio) to her apartment, where they make love and discuss how miserable Mauricio and Vera will be now that they must return to their mundane lives. They conclude, while they are dividing and swallowing fatal tablets, that the married couple must commit suicide rather than face their inevitable unhappiness.

"Trade Winds" has a good deal in common with Cortázar's classic stories of the fantastic. It is carefully structured; the ending is a surprise, yet inevitable in retrospect. Here, however, the couple's downfall is not due to any mysterious "other" force, but follows from the rules that they themselves establish. Moreover, Vera and Mauricio do not actually become Anna and Sandro in a case of transmigration, nor are they clearly sets of doubles, as in "Lejana" ("The Distances"). They are simply so taken with the game that they refuse to let it end. Even so, their rules are no more arbitrary than those of conventional society. All of Cortázar's rule-dominated stories reflect his personal rejection of stultifying conventionality.

While these two "game" stories are reminiscent of the fantastic, two mysteries based on political themes are quite similar to Cortázar's realistic stories. In "Pesadillas" (Nightmares),[30] one of his more overtly political pieces, a twenty-year-old woman, Mecha, lies in a coma, watched over by her parents and her brother. Despite the fact that the city is at war (Alazraki argues that Mecha's coma is Argentina's coma from 1976 to 1982),[31] punctuated by sirens and machine-gun fire, Lauro, the brother, is taking exams at the university. Whenever shots or sirens are heard, Mecha appears to be having nightmares, which worsen when Lauro is at hand. One night Lauro fails to come home, and the battles surround the neighborhood. Mecha finally awakens from her coma "a la hermosa vida" (to beautiful life) just as the door is being smashed in—one assumes by the police.

"Pesadillas" is quite similar to many stories of the Third World, dealing, as it does, with the themes of revolution, the "desaparecidos" (the disappeared) and government repression. In fact, it will remind many readers of the stories of Lino Novás Calvo and Guillermo Cabrera Infante, both important Cuban authors, although it is not nearly so good as their best works. The mother and father are clearly intended to be model citizens; Lauro is presumably involved in antigovernment activities, and, as Mecha means "fuse" in Spanish, the comatose woman is obviously symbolic.

Far more satisfying, at least in an aesthetic sense, is "La escuela de noche" (The school by night), also from the collection *Deshoras*.[32] Two students, Nito and Toto, both roughly of high-school age, decide to break into their school one night. Inside they discover a strange party is going on, attended by all of the more unpleasant faculty and students. The director, for example, is present, dressed as a woman. The two young men observe all sorts of perverse activities: a small dog is tied up and thrown into an aquarium filled with piranhas; the school's only female teacher, Maggie, locks Toto's head into an eye-examining device and masturbates him; all present beat one student while they recite a decalogue that stresses power and obedience to authority. Toto, the narrator, finally escapes. On Monday, when he hopes to denounce everyone, his best friend, Nito, warns him that if he does his life will be in danger. Nito has been won over to the other side.[33] Toto's conclusion that one day all of these unsavory individuals will rise up in service of the country makes Cortázar's point perfectly clear.

Cortázar insisted on the validity of the characters in this story:

All that is presumptuous, all that is pedantic, all that is pompous, precisely because I
saw it, I lived it, and I suffered it so much in Argentina. I hate it deeply. I had to endure an education in which many of my professors were blowhards, but pompous
and pedantic. And the serious thing is that I was sensible enough to recognize immediately that they were blowhards. That created a sense of rejection, because I felt I was
wasting my time with those people. The story "La escuela de noche" condenses, in a
way, that feeling. I grew up in a family many of whose members were also blowhards
with regard to ideas, or rather the lack of ideas. That is to say, people who imposed
their authority simply because they were older. Something I could never stand, that I
could never endure.[34]

Cortázar's wrath is deeply felt in the story, and indeed, as in the case of
"Pesadillas," his emotion seems to interfere with aesthetic development.
These two works, though presumably from late in the author's career, are
not up to the standard of his best stories. He seems to have gone from
using his fiction as therapy for his neuroses to exploiting it to vent his
anger and frustration.

An additional story published late in Cortázar's career also compares
unfavorably with his best work, and, as is often the case, was actually written much earlier. The author himself provided a preliminary note in which
he recognizes that "La barca o nueva visita a Venecia" ("The Ferry, or Another Trip to Venice")[35] is a bad story that he first wrote in 1954. Ten years
later, he rediscovered it and thought it bad, but still liked it. Ten more years
passed, and he still liked it, although he still thought it bad. After
intercutting some newly written commentary on the story, made by one of
the characters, and providing the preliminary note of explanation, he published the piece in 1977.

The material that comprised the original tells of two friends, Valentina
and Dora, who are touring Italy. Valentina, involved in an affair with
Adriano, breaks off with him and goes on to Venice alone. There she has a
sudden and passionate sexual affair with a gondolier. When Adriano follows
her to Venice, she refuses to resume their relationship, although she does go
for a walk with him, allowing her gondolier lover to see her. Presumably, both
ties are broken.

The intercut material that Cortázar added later is all provided by
Valentina's friend, Dora, who shows her jealousy and resentment of
Valentina, hints at her lesbian sexuality, interferes with Valentina's plans, and
apparently overdoses on Valium at the end of the story.[36] Her comments on
Valentina, however, are far less interesting than her comments on the story it-
self and on Cortázar's narration: "La opción ya tomada, se hace pensar como

se quiere a Valentina, pero otras opciones son posibles si se tiene en cuenta que ella optó por irse *sola* a Venecia" ("Having taken a choice, he makes Valentina think the way he wants, but other choices are possible if one keeps in mind the fact that she opted to go to Venice *alone*" [*Relatos* 3:63; *We Love Glenda* 354]); "Cuánto artificio barato, después de todo. Se hace hablar y pensar a Valentina cuando se trata de tonterías; lo otro, silencio o atribuciones casi siempre dirigidas en la mala dirección. ¿Por qué no escuchamos lo que Valentina pudo murmurar antes de dormirse" ("So many cheap tricks, after all. Valentina is made to speak and think when it's a matter of foolishness; otherwise, silence or attributions almost always aimed in the wrong direction. Why don't we hear more of what Valentina might have murmured before falling asleep" [65–66; 358]). In short, Cortázar has taken some of the story's weaknesses, given one of the characters life outside of the narrative, and allowed her to comment on the story and on its composition, thus turning weakness into strength. While this device certainly improves the work, the story remains weak.

"Historia con migalas" ("Story with Spiders"),[37] although a much better story, seems excessively vague. It tells of what appear to be two individuals (the narration is in the first person "we") who take a Christmas holiday on a remote corner of an equally remote island in the Caribbean. They hope to be absolutely alone, but find that the other end of their double bungalow is occupied by two young American women. The protagonists become accustomed to listening to the murmur of the women's quiet conversations, but one evening hear the distinct voice of a man. As the uneventful days slowly pass, it becomes evident that the protagonists have come to the island to escape, and that their flight was precipitated by events that are communicated only through fragments of detail: Eric's farm, nighttime, Michael running naked in the moonlight, a well. Now they simply wait, like spiders in the dark, thinking that "la noche de la granja valió el precio que estamos pagando" ("the night on the farm was worth the price we're paying" [*Relatos* 2:27; *We Love Glenda* 21]).

When the two American tourists leave, the "we" protagonists explore their end of the bungalow. At night they seem to hear a man's cough coming from the vacant end of the building, a cough that reminds them again of Michael: "cómo también Michael volvió a la granja de Erik, sin ninguna razón aparente volvió aunque para él la granja ya estaba vacía como el bungalow de al lado, volvió como ha vuelto el visitante de las muchachas, igual que Michael y los otros volviendo como las moscas, volviendo sin saber que se los espera, que esta vez vienen a una cita diferente" ("how Michael too went back to Erik's farm, went back with no apparent reason, even though the farmhouse for him was as empty as the wing of the bungalow next door, came back just as the girls' visitor has come back, just like Michael and the others, coming back like flies, coming back without knowing that they're expected, that this time they're coming to a different appointment" [33; 28]). In the final line, after the protagonists have undressed and slipped into the bungalow where they have heard the man, the reader learns they are females: "nos apoyamos la una en la otra para andar" ("we lean on each other in order to walk" [33; 29]). This question of gender, discernible only in the Spanish version, yet carefully disguised by the author until the final line, forces the reader to reconsider the entire story, which has seemed at moments to be an account of paid assassins who are waiting for the furor to die down from their last murder. The final scene, however, with its allusions to dark corners, nighttime, returning flies, and the sudden revelation that the protagonists are women, suggests that they are spider women, ever waiting in the darkness to entrap and devour men. After a first reading, one almost wants to believe that the protagonists are in fact arachnids, but then one remembers that they smoke cigarettes, drink wine, rent bungalows, and wear clothing.

The mystery is almost as deep in "Después del almuerzo" (After lunch),[38] which in many ways should be considered a psychological story. The first-person narrator, a child, is forced by his parents to take "him" or "it" for a walk after lunch. Immediately "he" gets all muddy; then they are unable to sit together on the streetcar, and the narrator is terrified that "he" will make a scene ("he" evidently created an uproar involving a neighbor's cat in the past). Once downtown, the narrator abandons his burden on a park bench, but after a long walk his sense of guilt makes him return, where with a mixture of relief and dismay he finds "him" still waiting patiently. The narrator silently wonders if either of his parents ever suffered the temptation to abandon the creature somewhere.

The mysterious element in "Después del almuerzo" is clearly the identity, or the nature of "him" ("it"?). In many ways, "it" appears to be a pet, a family dog, etc., but such a reading makes incongruous the boy's embarrassment at being seen in public with "it" and the fact that "he" can sit on a streetcar seat, often without even attracting attention. Only when "he" misbehaves are there problems. The most logical explanation is that "he" is a retarded member of the family, in which case the story becomes an excellent study of child psychology as it explores the narrator's conflicting feelings of reluctance and obedience, embarrassment and responsibility, guilt and duty. In the end he complies with his responsibility, rescuing and returning "him" safely home.

The psychological agony of the streetcar ride in "Después del almuerzo" highlights the significance of public transportation in Cortázar's fiction. The bus, the subway, the streetcar, the ship all provide opportunities to meet others, as in "Throat of a Black Kitten" and "Manuscript Found in a Pocket," enclosed spaces in which to pursue one's victims, as in "El móvil," passages to adventure or another life, as in "The Ferry, or Another Trip to Venice," or encounters with destiny, as in "A Yellow Flower".

In this vein, "Texto en una libreta" ("Text in a Notebook")[39] explores the secret world of the subway system in the style of vintage Cortázar. The narrator discovers (imagines?), through analyses of the discrepancies in the count of passengers boarding and exiting the subway on certain days, that a number of individuals actually live in the system. He dedicates hours, days, and weeks to riding the trains, studying those he believes to be part of this secret society. He determines that they are taking over more and more trains, and that their plan is to control one day the entire subway system. Finally, he believes that they identify him as a threat, as the one who will expose their plot. He flees into a cafe, where he writes out what he has learned, the text in a notebook. As in the case of the manuscript found in a pocket, the reader senses that the author of this text, which is still in notebook form, is now deceased; that indeed the secret subway society has eliminated another threat to its future.

Like "Después del almuerzo," "Text in a Notebook" can be viewed as a psychological story rather than a mystery. There is no proof that the narrator is destroyed by the subway people, just as there is nothing to verify that his discovery is more than the product of an overactive imagination. Another piece, "Los buenos servicios" ("At Your Service"),[40] also serves as a bridge between the mysterious and psychological. The first-person narrator, Madame Francinet, tells of how she was hired by a wealthy family to baby-sit their dogs during a party. After the party, one of the young men who attended, Bébé, is kind to her. Some time later, the family again employs Madame Francinet to attend the funeral of a friend. She is to pretend to be the mother of the deceased. When she approaches the casket, she discovers that the deceased is the same man who befriended her after the party. She plays her role so well that even her employers cannot tell whether she is acting or truly grieving. Meanwhile, a strange and threatening man appears at the funeral, making the reader feel concern that Madame Francinet will be exposed.

Madame Francinet is a simple, honorable woman, who will remind many readers of Félicité, in Flaubert's "A Simple Heart" (moreover, one of the characters is named Loulou, the same as Félicité's parrot). As Jaime Alazraki has pointed out, the success of "At Your Service" depends to a large degree upon having Madame Francinet narrate the story, for she cannot explain the events she observes.[41] Indeed, "Not only is she the only person who genuinely mourns Bébé's death, but also she is the sole character heedless of the fact that the men whom she met at the party, and again at the wake, are a group of homosexuals."[42]

These three stories, "Después del almuerzo," "Text in a Notebook," and "At Your Service," all have first-person narrators, and each is as interesting for the psychological exploration of the characters as for the mysterious events narrated. In fact, one of Cortázar's greatest strengths was his ability to capture the psychology of an individual or even a group in brief narrative forms.

Chapter Four
Short Stories: The Psychological

Many of Cortázar's stories have been analysed from psychological perspectives: often critics have explained the fantastic, "lo otro" (the other), as the mental aberrations of characters who have become temporarily or permanently deranged. Thus the rabbits in "Letter to a Young Lady in Paris" become hallucinations, "Blow-up" is simply the story of a protagonist gone mad, and the mancuspias in "Cefalea" become aspects of the main characters' psychotherapy.[1] Despite Cortázar's distaste for such readings, many have proved insightful. Unfortunately, far too often these interpretations deny the validity of other readings, equally valuable, that are premised upon the events narrated being "real," not hallucinatory. Cortázar clearly intended, and preferred, this latter approach.

Nonetheless, the author went to great pains to explore in depth the psychology of many of his characters; indeed, often this exploration seems to be a story's primary motivation. However, in all of these "psychological stories" it is unnecessary to interpret objects and events metaphorically, and hallucinations and delusions can typically be verified as such through information provided by the stories themselves. The dominant concerns of these works are isolation and death. Many deal with the traumas of childhood and adolescence, others with the equally traumatic years of adulthood and old age. Some isolate the individual, portraying him or her from within; others isolate and view from without. Still others explore the psychology of the group. The early stories are often hopeful, or wryly humorous; those of the later years tend to be increasingly pessimistic.

Cortázar's interest in psychology was evident even in his first collection, which contains two such stories. "Omnibus" (*Relatos* 1:149–59) has proved to be particularly attractive to metaphorical interpreters. In this story, a young woman, Clara, gets on a bus to go visit a friend. She soon observes that she is the only person on the bus without a bouquet of flowers (one of the final stops on the route is a large cemetery). Clara is keenly aware that all of the other passengers are staring at her. When, some time later, a young man gets on, also without flowers, attention shifts to him. At the cemetery, everyone but these two gets off the bus. The conductor repeats the name of the stop loudly, as if insisting that they too should leave the bus, but they insist they are going on. From time to time the conductor, seemingly enraged, acts as if he is going to throw them off physically, but the guard restrains him. Clara and the young man, now bound together by the bonds of shared persecution, plan their escape at Retiro. When they suddenly jump off the bus, the conductor makes a grab for them, but misses. The young man buys flowers for Clara and for himself at the first flower stand.

"Omnibus" clearly provides fertile ground for metaphorical interpretations. Some critics have felt that Clara and the young man have somehow learned their lesson, and that the next time they catch that bus they will be carrying flowers and that they will number among the "aggressors."[2] Even Jaime Alazraki, certainly one of Cortázar's best critics, believes that the "normal" passengers are those with the flowers, and that Clara and her new friend are a fantastic intrusion that is resolved when they obtain their own bouquets.[3] Nonetheless, it makes perfect sense to read "Omnibus" as a psychologically accurate portrayal of what it is like to feel somehow out of place in a crowded public spot—on an elevator, in a restaurant, or, in this case, on a bus. Every glance seems a stare, every gesture a threat. Even the menacing conductor may be no more than a man who is angry because of a mere two passengers who insist on going to the end of the line, making it impossible for him to take the bus out of service at the cemetery. These same feelings of isolation and estrangement were explored in very similar terms in the mysterious "Después del almuezo" (After lunch). It is this psychological suffering, and its relief with the final "escape" of the characters, that most readers will remember long after the story is finished.

The other early psychological story, "Las puertas del cielo" ("The Gates of Heaven"),[4] deals with another of Cortázar's obsessive themes, death. The story begins as Dr. Marcelo Hardoy, a lawyer who serves as narrator, learns of the death of Celina, the wife of his close friend, Mauro. Hardoy does his best to comfort his friend, and, some time after the funeral, persuades him to go out to a dance club, the seedy sort of a club that Celina frequented before her marriage to Mauro. After a few drinks and dances, Hardoy and Mauro are spellbound by what appears to be Celina, dancing at the other end of the bar. Mauro goes after her, but Hardoy knows he will not find her.

One significant feature of "The Gates of Heaven" is the use of a secondary character as narrator. By employing Hardoy in this capacity, Cortázar is able to achieve maximum ambiguity with regard to the appearance of Celina, for he, as author, does not have to commit himself; she may have appeared or she may simply be the product of the collective imaginations of Hardoy and Mauro. As Alazraki has pointed out, if the narrator could explain events, the story would fail.[5] The story is also important because of its political fallout. The portrayal of the violent and jaded types who frequent the tango parlor visited by Hardoy and Mauro incurred the wrath of many Peronists even though Cortázar attributed the story's content to a "mistaken vision of the national phenomenon at that moment."[6] Nonetheless, Cortázar insisted that he personally had witnessed scenes such as those portrayed in the story. The accuracy of the portrayal, however, is far less important than the psychological portrait of the two friends and their shared vision.

One of Cortázar's greatest strengths as an artist was his ability to portray the psychology of children and adolescents, a talent he displayed masterfully in the title story of *Final del juego* (*End of the Game*).[7] "End of the Game" concerns three young girls, one of whom is crippled, that pose in a field as statues for the entertainment of passengers on the 2:08 train. Each day they draw lots to determine which one will be the statue; the two losers select costumes and jewelry. One day a young passenger, Ariel, drops a note from the window, expressing his appreciation for their efforts. After several more days and notes, some of which express the young man's preference for the statues of Letitia, the crippled girl, their admirer announces that he is going to get off at their town so he can visit with them for a while. Letitia refuses to meet with him, but sends him a letter by way of the other girls. On the following day, Letitia poses, tears streaming from her eyes, and the young man stares from the train window for the last time. The next day Letitia is too ill to go to the tracks, and Ariel's face is no longer visible on the train. Presumably he now sits on the other side of the car, gazing out the opposite window.

The power of "End of the Game" derives from Cortázar's ability to capture the spirit of the three girls, which in turn is dependent upon his decision to use one of the three as narrator. This choice of narrative voice is perfect for rendering the story, for the narrator does not fully comprehend or appreciate all events. This limited understanding is thus all that is shared with the reader, who is forced to become, as it were, another child within the story.

Narrative voice is equally critical in "Los venenos" (Poisons), one of Cortázar's classic studies in juvenile psychology.[8] The narrator, a young adolescent, eagerly awaits the arrival of a new machine that is to be used to kill ants. He is disappointed by the device's appearance, but its ample weight restores his confidence, and his pride receives a boost when it is made clear that for safety's sake his younger sister will not be allowed to help in the extermination. On the first test run, the machine functions perfectly, and the narrator busily helps his uncle operate it, using mud to seal off all avenues of escape for the poisonous smoke: "yo me puse al lado de él con las manos llenas de barro hasta los codos, y se veía que era un trabajo para que lo hicieran los hombres" (I positioned myself alongside him with my hands covered with mud up to the elbows, and one could see that that was a job for men [*Relatos* 2:79]). The extermination project is delayed for several days during which the narrator's cousin, Hugo, pays a visit. Not only does Hugo arouse a good deal of jealousy in the narrator, he quickly enamors his younger sister. During one of the children's games, the neighbor girl, with whom the narrator is infatuated, injures her knee. As the protagonist doctors the wound, he notices how bravely she looks at Hugo, without crying. With his juvenile love inflamed even more by Lila's bravery, he digs up his jasmine plant, gives it to her, and helps her plant it in her own garden. When the ant fumigator is again pressed into service, after Hugo has returned to Buenos Aires, the poisonous smoke works its way through the underground passageways to the jasmine plant. As the narrator struggles to save the tree, he discovers that Lila now has Hugo's most prized possession, a peacock feather that he refused to give to the other children. Infuriated, he leaps back into his own yard, "abrí la lata del veneno y eché dos, tres cucharadas llenas en la máquina y la cerré; así el humo invadía bien los hormigueros y mataba todas las hormigas, no dejaba ni una hormiga viva en el jardín de casa" (I opened the can of poison and I threw two, three heaping spoonfuls into the machine and closed it up; thus the smoke thoroughly invaded the ant hills and killed all the ants, leaving not a single ant alive in the garden [89]).

Such a gloss cannot begin to do justice to the many nuances of infantile jealousy and pride that Cortázar captures through his careful manipulation of language. Line after line, paragraph upon paragraph, he seems to have discovered the exact phrasing to recreate these sensations in his readers. The story overtly narrated is but a superficial beginning, for many equally interesting stories flow beneath its surface. One key to the success of such works is the depth to which the author himself identified with his juvenile protagonists: "The depth of sensibility of the girl, Isabel, in 'Bestiary' is mine, and the boy in 'Los venenos' is me. In general, the children that move about in my stories represent me in some way."9

While "End of the Game" and "Los venenos," both from the same collection, are arguably the stories in which Cortázar best reveals this sensitivity, his interest in the theme carries over into later collections as well. In "La señorita Cora" ("Nurse Cora")10 the protagonist is a bit older (fifteen), but equally sensitive, especially with regard to his budding adulthood.

In reality, "Nurse Cora" has two protagonists, the young patient, hospitalized for an appendectomy, and his youthful nurse. The patient, Pablo, has been badly spoiled by his doting mother, who hovers over him in the hospital, to his great embarrassment. He finds Cora most attractive, but his request to call her by her given name is coldly rejected. From that moment on, the two are constantly at odds: he is humiliated by such routine hospital procedures as temperature taking and bathing, for he wants to show his manhood and strength, while she seems bent on increasing his embarrassment and keeping him in his place. The surgery does not go well; an infection develops, and high fever and pain set in. Cora, suddenly concerned for her ward's life, reverses her attitude, now remaining constantly at his side and comforting him. However, when she begs him to call her Cora, shortly before his death, he steadfastly refuses.

"Nurse Cora" is an ambitious experiment, for not only does it develop the psychological crisis of two protagonists in a relatively brief space, it changes perspective a total of thirty-four times. The dominant perspectives are those of the two main characters, but others are also represented. The story opens, for example, with the voice of the hovering mother: "No entiendo por qué no me dejan pasar la noche en la clínica con el nene, al fin y al cabo soy su madre" ("I can't understand why they don't let me spend the night in the hospital with the baby, after all I'm his mother" [*Relatos* 2:207; *All Fires* 65]). As in those fantastic stories in which two realities are gradually fused, this initial orientation is clear for several lines. However, before even the first paragraph is finished, the perspective switches to that of Pablo: "Habrá que ver si la frazada lo abriga bien al nene, voy a pedir que por las dudas le dejen otra a mano. Pero sí, claro que me abriga" ("I wonder if the baby's warm enough with that blanket, just to be sure I'll ask them to leave another one in reach. Of course I'm warm enough" [207; 66]). As this quote indicates, not only is the perspective constantly shifting, but the changes often come in the middle of an event or idea, with one character finishing what another has begun, even if what is completed is a thought.

The transitions, which link thirty-five clearly definable segments over a span of only eighteen paragraphs, are much akin to the bridges used in jazz, and given Cortázar's affinity for that musical form and its incorporation into many of his major works, especially *Rayuela* (*Hopscotch*) and "El perseguidor" ("The Pursuer"), both predecessors of "Nurse Cora," one may assume that the similarity is deliberate. The major "instruments" in this case are the mother, Pablo, Cora, and Cora's boyfriend, Marcial, who also serves as Pablo's anesthesiologist. In addition to the eighteen paragraphs, the story is broken into six major elements: 1) before the initial surgery; 2) immediately after the operation; 3) complications, Cora begins to soften somewhat; 4) Pablo's condition worsens and Cora continues to weaken; 5) Pablo's perspective dominates as he grows increasingly feverish; 6) now Cora's perspective is dominant, a second operation is performed, and Pablo dies. If textual extension (the number of lines devoted to a particular theme, character, or perspective) is any measure, the domination of the mother at the beginning yields to the struggle between Cora and Pablo, and Pablo emerges as a man only when he is on the brink of death.

Adolescent psychology is also the focus of "Siestas,"[11] one of the many stories included in *Ultimo round*. Two pubescent girls, Teresa and Wanda, take advantage of the siesta hour to listen to jazz recordings by Billie Holiday, view erotic art in the study of Teresa's father, smoke, and make sexual explorations of themselves and each other. Wanda, the protagonist, is troubled by nightmares in which she is attacked by a man with an artificial hand. The dream's origin is unclear, "la mezcla de recuerdos del otro verano y la pesadilla, el hombre que se parecía tanto a los del álbum del padre de Teresita, o el callejón sin salida donde al anochecer el hombre de negro la había acorralado" (the mixture of memories from last summer and nightmare, the man who looked so much like those in the album of Teresita's father, or the blind alley where one evening at dusk the man in black had cornered her [*Relatos* 1:88; my translation]).

Much of the story is devoted to the girls' sexual explorations. When Wanda continues these activities in her own home, alone, she is caught and severely punished, thus increasing her sense of shame and guilt. The pictures in the album at Teresa's are also troubling to Wanda.[12] They depict individuals, nude or only partially clothed, wandering about through gardens and along streets as if such behavior were normal. Wanda's guilt and confusion drive her to thoughts of suicide, as the visions of the dream, the album, and the experience with the man in the alley (presumably a real experience) coalesce.

The ending of "Siestas" is ambiguous. The final paragraph is a fusion of images: the album, the man with the artificial hand, the alley, sexual explorations with Teresa, punishment, the kindness of Wanda's only benefactor, her aunt Lorenza. Gyurko believes Wanda goes mad, and the dream becomes her reality,[13] but it is equally possible that she simply slips into her nightmare, under the influence of a tonic administered by her kindly aunt: "—Bebé un poco más—dijo tía Lorenza—. Ahora vas a dormir hasta mañana sin soñar nada" ("Drink a little more," said Aunt Lorenza. "Now you are going to sleep until tomorrow without dreaming at all" [98]). The omission of this paragraph in the Christensen translation (286) makes the ending particularly problematic in the English version. What is most significant in "Siestas" is the mastery with which Cortázar conveys the damage done to young psyches by domineering, puritanical adults. The healthy child is clearly Teresa, even though her parents allow her so much freedom that she has been banished from Wanda's house and she is systematically blamed for leading Wanda astray.

The portrayal of the two households embodies another of Cortázar's great strengths, the ability to capture and convey the psychology of a group, a skill which is particularly evident in three stories: "Cartas de mamá" (Letters from Mama), "La salud de los enfermos" ("The Health of the Sick"), and "Las ménades" (The maenads).[14]

"Las ménades" is in many ways the least interesting of the three, at least in psychological terms. A bored man goes to a concert, to be led by a vastly overrated conductor. The program is predictably chaotic, and as mediocre as the protagonist anticipated. However, he is informed, this is the conductor's twenty-fifth anniversary with the orchestra, and each of the pieces has been requested by the audience. Oddly enough, the audience is enraptured with the performance, and at intermission the protagonist must listen to choruses of effusive, though undeserved, praise. At the end of the concert the audience is engulfed in a wave of collective hysteria. The thunderous applause culminates in members of the audience actually storming the stage, carrying off the performers, and destroying their instruments. This madness, which is led by "la mujer roja y sus seguidores" (the woman in red and her followers [*Relatos* 1:194]), is extremely orgiastic ("ménades" are "maenads" or bacchantes), with echoes of cannibalism, as suggested by the woman in red who at the end "se pasaba la lengua por los labios, lenta y golosamente se pasaba la lengua por los labios que sonreían" (licked her lips with her tongue, slowly and hungrily licked her smiling lips [199]). This cannibalism is only suggested metaphorically, however. On a much more immediate level the story satirizes a tasteless public's blind adulation of mediocre artists and their work, or what Alazraki has termed "the paroxismal admiration for an artist that borders on . . . collective hysteria."[15]

The other two stories are far more significant to the Cortázar canon. The focus for "Cartas de mamá" is a married couple living in Paris. Laura was originally the girlfriend of Nico, the brother of her husband, Luis. Laura and Luis became involved with each other even before the death of Nico, two years before the story takes place. Their sudden marriage, immediately on the heels of Nico's death, angered Luis's family, so now the couple lives in virtual exile, with contact only through their correspondence with Luis's mother. Suddenly Mamá begins to mention Nico as if he were alive, and tells the couple of the dead brother's plans to visit them in Paris. Luis hides the first letter from Laura, but the references continue in the next letter as well.

The couple decides that Mamá is senile, and that the best thing is simply to ignore the Nico affair. Nonetheless, Luis goes to the station to see his brother arrive and notices Laura is also there. Both observe a man who indeed resembles Nico, but, as they later comment, is somewhat thinner.

Most critics seem to have taken the arrival of Nico literally, although it is difficult to fathom their reasons. As Elvira Aguirre has pointed out, virtually all information is subjective, obtained from letters, and reflexive: "The reflexive narration, whose theme, properly, is subjectivity, reveals how this subjectivity loses its shape with each new letter from the mother, letters that are, naturally, the point of reference for the subject [Luis and Laura]."[16] What is incontrovertible is the conclusion almost all critics have reached, that Luis and Laura suffer from intense guilt, and that their guilt is greatly heightened by the letters. Whether Luis actually goes mad, whether the two share a hallucinated vision of Nico at the station, or whether, as may be the case in "The Gates of Heaven," they simply see someone who resembles the dead person and accept the vision as such, is impossible to determine. As so often in Cortázar, rigid adherence to any one of these readings weakens the aesthetic ambiguity of the story. More important, in terms of what is "real," is the sense of guilt of the couple and their relationship with what may well be an accusing, tormenting mother.

Family relations are much more positive in "The Health of the Sick," one of Cortázar's masterpieces. In this case, an entire family goes far out of its way to protect the one member they feel is least capable of dealing with a crisis. When Alejandro is killed in a car wreck, his aunts and uncles, brothers and sisters, and even his fiancée conspire to protect his mother from the news. Newspapers that would notify her of the accident or the funeral are confiscated. An elaborate scheme, in which Alejandro has gone off to Brazil to work, is set up. A family friend in Brazil receives letters that the family writes for the fictitious Alejandro and then mails them to Mamá. Business and political crises and even a broken leg are used to explain the delay in the son's return. Meanwhile there is reason to suspect that Mamá is on to them all. She wonders aloud why Alejandro always types his letters instead of writing them longhand, and she expresses her dissatisfaction that he never calls her by her secret name. Convinced that Mamá knows the truth, María Laura, the fiancée, can no longer bear to come to visit. The situation worsens when Aunt Clelia falls ill and they now have to protect Mamá from two pieces of bad news. Aunt Clelia is supposedly sent to their country place, from which comes daily news of her improving health, even after she too has died. When the end finally comes for Mamá they discover that María Laura's suspicions were correct, for Mamá thanks them all for being so good and protective. The pretense has left its residue, however:

Tres días después del entierro llegó la última carta de Alejandro, donde como siempre preguntaba por la salud de mamá y de tía Clelia. Rosa, que la había recibido, la abrió y empezó a leerla sin pensar, y cuando levantó la vista porque de golpe las lágrimas la cegaban, se dio cuenta de que mientras la leía había estado pensando en cómo habría que darle a Alejandro la noticia de la muerte de mamá.

(Three days after the funeral, Alejandro's last letter arrived, in which, as always, he asked about Mama's and Aunt Clelia's health. Rosa opened it and began reading without a second thought, and when she raised her eyes because they were suddenly blinded with tears, she realized that while she was reading, she had been thinking about how she was going to break the news to Alejandro that Mama was dead. [*Relatos* 3:167; *All Fires* 48])

Some critics have taken this paragraph as proof that Alejandro is indeed alive, just as some believe that Nico has been resurrected in "Cartas de mamá." The conclusion of "The Health of the Sick" is far less ambiguous, however, for it is clear that Rosa and the others have played the elaborate game of Alejandro's difficulties in Brazil for so long that he has taken on a sort of second life in their minds. Now that Mamá is dead, Alejandro and Aunt Clelia can also be laid to rest, but it will take time for the surviving family members to make the adjustment.

Particularly significant in this story is the positive portrayal of familial relationships. No character seeks to dominate or punish any other; all conspire for the good of Mamá, who is viewed as the most vulnerable of the group. The title cuts many ways: the sick, and even the dead, are kept alive for the sake of Mamá, but what may be viewed as an unhealthy effort to shield her from reality proves to be quite salubrious not only for her but for the entire group. María Laura's suspicions, given credence by Mamá's attempts to test the family with references to the composition of the letters and the secret names, and the dreaded recognition by all that all Mamá need do to collapse the entire house of cards is ask to speak to Aunt Clelia on the phone, prove correct. What matters is not who lives and who has died but the mutual support of the family, something that is unusual in Cortázar's stories.

While many of Cortázar's works explore the isolation of the individual as seen from within, only a few develop interpersonal relationships in a positive way, and fewer still depict isolation as seen from without. Certainly one of his most significant stories in this vein is the one many critics consider his best, "El perseguidor" ("The Pursuer").[17] This work, which is almost more novella than story, concerns two characters. Most critics see the protagonist as Johnny Carter, a brilliant jazz saxophonist whose life is destroyed and tragically ended by his drug addiction and incumbent psychological problems. Equally important from an artistic point of view, however, is the narrator, Bruno, who is Johnny's biographer and supposed friend. As Lanin A. Gyurko has pointed out, Bruno, although he seems to try to help Johnny at critical moments, is guilty of exploiting him.[18]

The character of Johnny is based on the legendary saxophonist, Charlie Parker. In fact, Robert W. Felkel has demonstrated that Cortázar changed few, if any, of the known facts about Parker's life.[19] The bulk of the story deals with a period during which Johnny, already in severe decline personally, although perhaps at his peak musically, was in Paris. He is the pursuer of the title, although he is unable to communicate to others precisely what he seeks, glimpsing it only in certain magical moments when he seems to exist outside of time, moments that may occur while he is playing or even while riding the subway. Bruno observes, "He visto pocos hombres tan preocupados por todo lo que se refiere al tiempo" ("I've seen very few men as occupied as he is with everything having to do with time" [*Relatos* 3:223; *Blow-up* 164]). Johnny, on the other hand, chides Bruno: "Tú no haces más que contar el tiempo" (You don't do anything but count time [221; my translation]). Illustrative of the saxophonist's quest is his statement, when he is playing particularly well and happily, "Esto lo estoy tocando mañana" ("I'm playing this tomorrow" [223; 164]).

Johnny's tormented life is only half the story; the other half is Bruno's observation, interpretation, and at times involvement in it. Although a jazz critic, he does not share the musician's euphoria or his insights. He feels superior in many ways to his subject, and his concern is often motivated by self-interest: "El fracaso de Johnny sería malo para mi libro" (If Johnny failed it would be bad for my book [240; my translation]). His sense of duty as a critic is at odds with his obligations to Carter as a friend. One of the saxophonist's greatest artistic moments is his studio rendition of "Amorous," but he hates the recording to such a degree that he makes the technicians swear they have destroyed the master. They deceive him, and so Bruno gets to hear the session, even though he knows Johnny wanted it destroyed: "Vaya a saber si *Amorous* no resulta el testamento del pobre Johnny; y en ese caso, mi deber profesional . . ." ("To see if *Amorous* would turn out to be Johnny's last will and testament. In which case, my professional duty would be . . ." [245;188]). Once Bruno hears the recording, he realizes that Johnny is not a victim, a man pursued, as he had portrayed him in his biography, but a pursuer, although there is no way to discover what he seeks (252–53; 196).

The recording is released, to the great satisfaction of Johnny's fans, but to his immense displeasure. His relationship with Bruno has finally reached the breaking point. Bruno goes back to "la vida de un crítico, ese hombre que sólo puede vivir de prestado, de las novedades y las decisiones ajenas" (the life of a critic, the man who can live only at another's expense, on new developments and decisions made by others [257; my translation]). After a few weeks Johnny apologizes and their "friendship" is renewed, allowing Bruno to observe that "mi superioridad frente a Johnny me ha permitido mostrarme indulgente" ("my superiority to Johnny allowed me to be indulgent" [261; 205]).

Eventually the two men discuss the biography. Carter believes it to be inaccurate, much to Bruno's pique, but the critic's concern is less the inaccuracies than the negative effect Johnny may have on sales if he denounces the book (263; 208). He admits to falsification, but for positive reasons: "Sé muy bien que el libro no dice la verdad sobre Johnny (tampoco miente), sino que no he querido mostrar al desnudo su incurable esquizofrenia, el sórdido trasfondo de la droga, la promiscuidad de esa vida lamentable" (I know perfectly well that the book does not tell the truth about Johnny (nor does it lie), but I did not want to lay bare his incurable schizophrenia, the sordid background of drugs, the promiscuity of that lamentable life [265–66; my translation]). Johnny, however, points out that "de lo que te has olvidado es de mí" ("what you forgot to put in is me" [266; 212]). Johnny Carter is to be found only in his music, on his records. What others hear is not his problem: "Si cuando yo toco tú ves a los ángeles, no es culpa mía" ("If I play and you see angels, that's not my fault" [268; 213]).

This lengthy debate notwithstanding, the second edition of the biography is left unchanged by Johnny's critique. Just before its publication, Carter dies. Bruno's reaction is that "por suerte tuve tiempo de incorporar una nota necrológica redactada a toda máquina, y una fotografía del entierro donde se veía a muchos jazzmen famosos. En esa forma la biografía quedó, por decirlo así, completa" ("luckily I had time to incorporate an obituary note edited under full steam and inserted, along with a newsphoto of the funeral in which many famous jazzmen were identifiable. In that format the biography remained, so to speak, intact and finished" [274; 220]).

"The Pursuer" is a watershed story for Cortázar. The author himself pointed out that in most of his previous works the characters were subservient to the action. Although in some stories (many of which have been discussed in this chapter) characters were presented with human complexity and depth, the first time "the dialogue, the confrontation with another, with someone who is not my [Cortázar's] double, but another human being who is not placed at the service of a fantastic story, where the story is the character, contains the character, is determined by the character, was in 'The Pursuer.'"[20] In other words, here Cortázar tried to get inside of his characters, both Bruno and Johnny Carter.[21] Not all critics reacted favorably to the attempt.[22] Cortázar, however, believed the story to be a miniature *Hopscotch*, and that he could never have written the latter without first creating the former.[23] Néstor García Canclini argues that "If one wants to learn to be a pursuer, one must read *Hopscotch*."[24] "The Pursuer" is not only Cortázar's longest story, but one of his most important.

One significant aspect of the story is that in addition to attempting to "get inside" his characters, Cortázar selected Bruno as narrator, thus making the critic the only one he could explore from within. He then had to portray the complexities of Johnny while restricting himself to the knowledge and understanding of Bruno. In doing so, he developed a great sensitivity to nuances of Johnny's actions and statements, a sensitivity that enabled him to communicate the essence of Johnny as effectively as he conveyed the inner truth of Bruno.

This remarkable power surfaces again in a much shorter, and considerably less important story, "El viaje" ("The Journey").[25] "The Journey" is an excellent and amusing story of a man, who, accompanied by his wife, attempts to buy a train ticket to go from Chaves to Peúlco, then on to Mercedes. He is to drive to Chaves, following an itinerary given to him by his boss, but by the time he gets to the ticket office, he is unable to remember the names of any of the towns. His wife is of no help whatsoever. They use a variety of methods to try to recall the correct names, going through letters of the alphabet, studying maps, checking distances and driving times, etc., but even when they hit upon the correct names, they are unable to recognize them. In the end, they appear to have guessed right, but, as the ticket clerk says, "Sería una lástima que al final se hubiera equivocado, ¿no?" ("It'd be too bad if after all that he was wrong, wouldn't it?" [*Relatos* 2:155; *Around the Day* 229]).

"The Journey" is interesting because of the dramatic presentation of the man and his wife. It is unusual because the perspective throughout is external to all of the characters; all is narrated as if by someone who was present in the train station when the couple arrived. The bulk of the story is dialogue, with only an introductory paragraph to set the scene and a few brief descriptions of the train station and the gestures and attitudes of the chief actors. Even so, the keen use of irony conveys precisely the strained relationship between the man and his wife. He seems rather old, and certainly worn from work (he is being sent by his company to Mercedes for a rest).

His tired patience, which borders on incompetence, is counterposed by her repressed anger, which she converts to seeming indifference and a decided contrariness. Before they arrived at the ticket office, when he tried to relate his conversation with his boss to his wife, she dryly remarked, "Sí, ya me contaste" (Yes, you already told me [146; my translation]); later, when he is struggling with the itinerary, she snips, "Yo no estaba cuando Juárez te explicó el viaje" ("I wasn't there when Juárez explained the trip to you" [148; 223]). At the end, after the ticket clerk expresses that it would be a shame if the man purchased the wrong ticket after all: "Casi en la puerta la mujer vuelve la cabeza y lo mira, pero la luz llega apenas hasta ella y ya es difícil saber si todavía se sonríe, si el golpe de la puerta al cerrarse lo ha dado ella o es el viento que se levanta casi siempre con la caída de la noche" ("Almost at the door, the woman turns her head and looks at him, but the light barely reaches her, and it's hard to tell if she is still smiling, if it is she who has caused the door to slam, or the wind, which almost always comes up at nightfall" [155; 229]). This is not to suggest that Cortázar's portrait of the woman is unsympathetic, for she is clearly at wit's end. The reader's delight in the story stems from the sympathetic and amusing rendering of both characters.

"The Journey" may have been written much earlier than its date of publication suggests, as in the cases of many stories from *Ultimo round* and *Around the Day in Eighty Worlds*. It is undeniable that beginning with the stories of *Octaedro* (Octahedron), Cortázar's humor is much darker and often absent altogether. Evelyn Picon Garfield, certainly one of the author's more devoted critics, subtitled her essay on *Octaedro* "Eight Phases of Despair," and prefaced her study with the observation that it had taken her many months to read the entire book because she found it so distressing.[26] Whether or not she is accurate in concluding that humor never played a major role in Cortázar's short fiction,[27] it is clear, as Marta Morello-Frosch also points out, that the characters seem more desperate, and that the games, verbal and otherwise, are now absent to a large degree.[28] Garfield concludes that Cortázar has been forced to return from his "other" reality to everyday reality, and in despair.[29]

The two stories from the collection that have been dealt with under the rubric of the fantastic, "Las fases de Severo" ("Severo's Phases") and "Verano" ("Summer") are far more ominous than many of the works in that category because they seem so immediate and "real." The mysteries, "Los pasos en las huellas" ("Footsteps in the Footprints"), "Manuscrito hallado en un bolsillo" ("Manuscript Found in a Pocket"), and "Cuello de gatito negro" ("Throat of a Black Kitten"), are also pessimistic treatments of dishonesty, violence, death, and despair.

The psychological stories too show a preoccupation with death, and a sense of despair with regard to interpersonal relationships. "Ahí pero dónde,

cómo" ("There But Where, How")³⁰ is particularly disturbing, for the narrator is clearly Cortázar himself, haunted by the death of a friend. The story
deals with his obsession with Paco, who died thirty years earlier, but unlike
other deceased friends, keeps returning through dreams and memories to
haunt him. He speculates that the reader too will have one death in his or her
past that continues to haunt. "There But Where, How" is extremely self-
conscious, and very like "Las babas del diablo" ("Blow-up"), as the following
selections indicate: "A vos que me leés, ¿no te habrá pasado eso que empieza
en un sueño y vuelve en muchos sueños pero no es eso, no es solamente en
sueño?" ("Those of you reading me, hasn't it happened to you, that thing that
starts as a dream and turns into many dreams but isn't that, isn't just a
dream?" [195; 381–82]); "Ya sé que no se puede escribir esto que.estoy
escribiendo, seguro que es otra de las maneras del día para terminar con las
débiles operaciones del sueño; ahora me iré a trabajar, me encontraré con
traductores y revisores en la conferencia de Ginebra donde estoy por cuatro
semanas . . . esta máquina que no servirá de nada ahora que estoy despierto y
sé que han pasado treinta y un años" ("I know that what I'm writing can't be
written, certain that it's another of the day's ways of ending the dream's weak
operations; now I'll go to work, I'll find myself among translators and editors
at the conference in Geneva where I've been for four weeks. . .this typewriter
that won't be good for anything now that I'm awake and know that thirty-
one years have gone by" [196; 383]); "No voy a perder más tiempo; si escribo
es porque sé, aunque no pueda explicarme qué es eso que sé" ("I'm not going
to waste any more time; if I write it's because I know, even if I can't explain
what it is I know" [197; 384]).

   While many of the phrases are almost verbatim from "Blow-up," this
story is far more serious, for it is about Cortázar and his friend Paco, to whom
Bestiario was dedicated some twenty-one years earlier. To verify this fact, the
original dedication serves as an epigraph to this story, and Cortázar reminds
his reader, as he often reminded his critics through interviews, that he actually
lived what many believed he had made up for his stories: "Y vos que me leés
creerás que invento; poco importa, hace mucho que la gente pone en la cuenta
de mi imaginación lo que de veras he vivido, o viceversa" ("And you who read
me will think that I'm inventing; it doesn't matter much, for a long time now
people have credited my imagination for what I've really lived or vice versa"
[202; 390]).

   "Liliana llorando" ("Liliana Weeping")³¹ is somewhat more positive, although it too deals with death. The narrator is a dying man who writes to
take his mind off his pain. His doctor is a close friend, whom he trusts to end
his life quickly once the pain becomes unbearable. As he imagines his death,

he continues beyond it, picturing how another friend, Arturo, will comfort and care for his wife, Liliana. In his mind (and on the page) he plays the scenario out over several weeks, until finally Arturo and Liliana, brought close by their months of companionship, kiss. When he returns to the reality of his sickbed, the narrator learns that Doctor Ramos was in error; his situation is not terminal. Just as he formerly prohibited Ramos from informing Liliana of the gravity of his illness so she would not suffer, he now forbids him to tell her he will live, for he does not want to destroy her newly found happiness (even though he imagined it).

Obviously, this story has much in common with "The Health of the Sick" in its portrayal of the sacrifices made by one human being on behalf of another, and in that sense must be viewed as a much more positive story than many of the others in this collection. In her essay, however, Garfield does not see it in that light, for she believes that the dream actually becomes the narrator's reality. Cortázar himself, however, argues that the denouement envisioned by the narrator is on another plane: "The dying man thinks out the future life of his wife, Liliana, over the course of many months—which for him are only two or three days in a hospital, writing—and, at the last moment, when he discovers that he is not going to die, Liliana's destiny, which was to find another man given of course that he would die, has already been fulfilled; it is fulfilled on another temporal plane, but it is fulfilled."[32]

The final psychological story from *Octaedro* is far more pessimistic, for its protagonist is as selfish and restrained as the narrator of "Liliana Weeping" is generous. "Lugar llamado Kindberg" ("A Place Named Kindberg")[33] shows the dominant male in his purest form. Marcelo, driving in Europe on business, picks up a pretty young hitchhiker. After a long day on the road, they take a room at an inn in Kindberg. The young woman, Lina, insists a single room with one bed is adequate, and spending the night making love seems quite natural to her. The following day, instead of going her own way, she tells him that she would like to ride with him for one more day. While he wants the pleasure of her company for another day (and perhaps night), he rejects her offer and goes on his way. He can see she is hurt by his rebuff. As he takes to the road he races his car furiously—until he crashes into a tree at eighty miles per hour.

The sharp contrast between the worlds of the two protagonists and their discussions of music suggest the validity of Garfield's interpretation: "Lina is spontaneous jazz, freedom adrift in the world, love that seeks no ties; and he is [a traveling salesman of prefabricated materials], who rejects Lina on his way to death."[34] Although Lanin A. Gyurko believes that Marcelo actually commits suicide because he cannot break out of his bourgeois mold and be-

come spontaneous like Lina,[35] it is equally likely that he is killed by his effort
to show off. It would be difficult to find either reading optimistic.

Three years after *Octaedro*, Cortázar published his next collection of stories, *Alguien que anda por allí*, which contains three psychological pieces. In
two, adults look at children in much the same way that the young viewed
the world of adults in the early stories. Only one of the three, however, has a
positive view of interpersonal relationships, "Usted se tendió a tu lado"
(You stretched out at thy side).[36] As the title suggests, Cortázar plays masterfully with personal pronouns—"usted" (the formal "you") and "vos" (the
familiar "you" used in Argentina). The mixture is confusing at first, but
provides the story with a depth of intimacy that could perhaps be achieved
in no other way. Cortázar explained the work as follows: "it departs from an
apparent grammatical mistake (you [usted] stretched out at *your* [tu] side,
instead of *his* side) where a third-person narrator tells the story of a mother
and her son and addresses the mother as *you* [usted] while using the informal "you" [tú] with the boy."[37] The grammatic mix is enriched by the fact
that Roberto, the son, alternates between calling his mother "mamá" and
"Denise." Once the reader discovers these textual peculiarities, such sentences as "Usted se tendió a tu lado y vos te enderezaste para buscar el
paquete de cigarrillos y el encendedor" (You [Denise] stretched out at your
[Roberto's] side and you [Roberto] stood up to look for the pack of cigarettes and the lighter [91]), and "Usted se levantó y la seguiste a unos pasos,
esperaste que se tirara al agua . . ." (You [Denise] got up and you [Roberto]
followed you [Denise], you [Roberto] waited until you [Denise] dived into
the water . . . [91]) are easy to follow, but it is also clear why the story has
not been translated into English.

The relationship between the two characters is particularly warm. As
mother and son vacation on the beach, Denise, concerned about Roberto's
budding romance with Lilian, who is equally young (about fifteen), and
about its possible consequences, purchases a packet of condoms for her son.
As she points out, however, her gift is more for Lilian's sake than for
Roberto's. Denise frequently and fondly remembers her son when he was still
her little boy, but she recognizes he is approaching manhood and she cannot
take care of him forever. The purchase of the condoms is also a cutting of
apron strings: "No tenemos más nada que decirnos, sabés que lo hice por
Lilian y no por vos. Ya que te sentís un hombre, aprendé a manejarte solo
ahora. Si al nene le duele la garganta, ya sabe dónde están las pastillas" (We
have nothing more to say to each other, you know that I did it for Lilian and
not for you. Now that you feel you are a man, learn to take care of yourself. If
sonny's throat hurts, he knows where the medicine is [98]).

While "Usted se tendió a tu lado" may be disorienting at first on a linguistic level, "En nombre de Boby" ("In the Name of Bobby")[38] is deeply disturbing and confusing in many ways. The title character is only eight years old, and suffers from nightmares in which his mother is cruel to him. He does not understand the difference between his dreams and reality, and is confused by the inconsistencies in his mother's behavior by day and by night. The story is narrated by Bobby's aunt, who also seems to imagine a great many dark and terrible things, but as in the case of the child's nightmares, these imaginings are never specified. She is especially preoccupied with the manner in which Bobby sometimes looks at his mother and the similar way in which he stares at the long kitchen knife. She becomes compulsive in making certain that the knife is properly put away out of sight. Eventually, Bobby's dreams end, but the stares remain. One day, evidently as a test, the aunt sends him into the house to fetch her the long knife. He returns with a short one instead, which she observes is useless. He throws himself into her arms and they embrace, weeping. The aunt, at last, understands, although it is unlikely that the reader will, even after careful study. Psychologically, the story seems quite valid in its capture of the mystery of dreams and obsessions. Precisely what the aunt glimpses at the conclusion is quite obscure, however. The suggestion is that Bobby used to imagine killing his mother, but that he no longer does. But that suggestion may stem from the aunt's admittedly active imagination.

No such confusion exists in "Las caras de la medalla" ("The Faces of the Medal"),[39] one of Cortázar's more depressing stories because of its grim, realistically drawn portrait of an unsuccessful love affair. Javier, who works as a temporary, travels to Geneva on a very irregular basis. His life with his companion, Eileen, is boring and in serious decline. In Geneva, in the offices where he occasionally works, he meets Mireille. Gradually, a relationship develops between them, but after months of what is practically a courtship, when she agrees to make love he is important. More months pass and the relationship continues to grow. When Javier is given another chance, the result is the same. After even more months he asks Mireille to go on vacation with him, but she refuses. After they stop seeing each other, she weeps occasionally, but he does not even know how.

As is the case in many of Cortázar's stories, narrative voice is an important aspect of "The Faces of the Medal." Sometimes the author employs third-person, sometimes first-person plural. While Javier is apparently a professional engineer, he is also a writer, and this is clearly one of his texts. He points out that his texts are like his nightmares—is "Faces of the Medal" a nightmare or an actual episode from his life? Like many of Cortázar's later stories, this work attempts far greater psychological depth than the early pieces. Unlike many others, "Faces of the Medal" is totally devoid of male domination, but it has been replaced by impotence rather than by a sense of balance. Also typical is the story's heightened sense of realism and its departure from the author's vintage explorations of the fantastic and the mysterious.

Cortázar's final collection of stories, *Deshoras* (Bad timing), contains one of his finer psychological stories, and one of his more positive. In the title piece, the first-person narrator, a writer, takes the reader back to his childhood in Bánfield, a suburb of Buenos Aires, to relate the story of Aníbal. Aníbal's closest childhood friend, Doro, is being raised by his sister, Sara. Aníbal falls in love with the much older Sara as only a child can fall in love: "nadie podía comprender esa pena y ese deseo de morir por Sara, de salvarla de un tigre o de un incendio y morir por ella, y que ella se lo agradeciera y lo besara llorando" (no one was capable of understanding that suffering and that desire to die for Sara, to save her from a tiger or from a fire and to die for her, and she would be grateful to him and would kiss him, crying [2: 232– 33]). One day, when Doro and Aníbal have gotten particularly filthy at play, Sara makes them undress and bathe. In the middle of their bath she comes in to wash them, to the total humiliation of Aníbal. Later, Sara marries and the two friends drift apart as they grow up, but years later Aníbal recognizes Sara in the street. He strikes up a conversation with her and they share a few drinks. Sara tells how her husband now has a problem with alcohol, and Aníbal confesses his childhood love and how she destroyed it with the bathing incident. She makes it clear that her feelings for him were equally strong, but he was five years too young for her. She interrupted the bath deliberately, to put an end to his dream.

The narrator imagines that Aníbal and Sara continue their conversation well into the night, and that they then finally consummate their love. As he imagines them smoking their last cigarette, the following dawn, he comes back to his own reality: "Cuando apagué la lámpara del escritorio y miré el fondo del vaso vacío, todo era todavía pura negación de las nueve de la noche, de la fatiga" (When I turned off the desk lamp and looked into the bottom of the empty glass, everything was still the pure negation of nine o'clock at night, of fatigue [241]). It becomes clear that the narrator is Aníbal, and that he still dreams of Sara, that he has written the story so he could dwell on her, that he longs to begin a life with her, but "cómo empezar desde esa noche una vida con Sara cuando ahí al lado se oía la voz de Felisa que entraba con los chicos y venía a decirme que la cena estaba pronta, que fuéramos en seguida a comer porque ya era tarde y los chicos querían ver al pato Donald en la televisión de las diez y veinte" (but how to begin from that night a life with

Sara when there, near by, one could hear the voice of Felisa who was coming in with the children and was coming to tell me that dinner was ready, that we must go eat quickly because it was already late and the children wanted to watch Donald Duck on television at ten twenty [24]).

"Deshoras" is a moving love story, perhaps the most touching story Cortázar ever wrote. It is particularly rewarding because it is devoid of the despair and pessimism that Garfield found so distressing in the earlier *Octaedro*. As Alicia Helda Puleo points out, this story "appears as a notable evocation of that total love that Cortázar's characters were never able to enjoy."[40] Jaime Alazraki is equally taken with "Deshoras," which he sees as the culmination of the theme of childhood/adolescence in Cortázar's works. He points out that the idealized consummation of Sara and Aníbal's love is both real and unreal; it takes place, but only on the literary plane.[41]

Any attempt to summarize, describe, capture the tone, or convey the emotion of one of Cortázar's stories is doomed to failure. The effort to do so is especially difficult in the psychological stories, and particularly in this brief masterpiece. Alazraki's lament regarding "Deshoras" has surely been echoed by every critic who has tried to explain Cortázar: "I reread what I have written and I realize that no description can ever explain the marvelous magic of that story."[42]

Chapter Five
Short Stories: The Realistic

The boundary that separates Cortázar's realistic stories from the psychological, the mysterious, or even the fantastic, is often a fine one indeed. The realistic works, however, tend to be more specific in describing the immediate setting, and more importantly, deal with situations that readers have encountered, if not in their own lives, certainly through newspapers and television. The elegance and beauty that are often found in a Cortázar story are here frequently replaced by a sense of the sordid and ugly. Whereas characters in "The Idol of the Cyclades" may lick stone axes and crouch in wait to murder friends and family in accordance with a supernatural dictum that has been passed on to them by a mysterious ancient icon, here they wait in automobiles to gun down old friends as they arrive at a restaurant, in accordance with orders from immediate superiors. When they have served their purposes, they too may be murdered.

The realistic stories are spread throughout Cortázar's career, although it is clear that they became far more important to him later in life, for only three of the ten pieces were published before 1977. The first two, "Torito" (Little bull)[1] and "Los amigos" (The friends)[2] already represent the two predominant themes of the stories in this group: violence (usually hand in hand with politics) and boxing.

"Los amigos" has received scant critical attention. Only three characters are involved, and but two actually appear, a murderer and his victim. The third ordered the killing. Romero and Beltrán are old friends who used to frequent the race track together. Now they are involved either in a political organization or in organized crime, and their code names reflect their ranks: Número Uno (Number one), who gives the order, Número Dos (Number two), who is to be killed, and Número Tres (Number three), the hit man. Número Tres (Beltrán) waits in his automobile outside the restaurant that Número Dos (Romero) frequents and guns him down when he arrives. As Beltrán drives away from the scene he reflects on how the last thing Romero had seen was the face of an old friend from the race track. While it shows Cortázar's interest in the theme of organized violence, "Los amigos" is inferior to the majority of his stories from the period in which it was written.

"Torito," however, is a much different case and deals with a different theme, professional boxing. In fact the qualitative difference between the two stories may be in part due to the author's reluctance to write "compromised" literature on the one hand, and his unrestrained love for boxing and for great prizefighters on the other. His interest in the sport is reflected in his other writings, particularly in "El noble arte" (The noble art)[3] and "Descripción de un combate o a buen entendedor" (Description of a fight, or to the well-initiated).[4] The first essay, in addition to showing his early interest in boxing, laments the fact that he witnessed both the birth of radio and the decline of boxing. One of the most vivid memories of his childhood was gathering around the radio to listen to the infamous fight between Luis Firpo and Jack Dempsey in 1923. Early in the contest, Firpo sent Dempsey through the ropes, and in clear violation of the rules fans helped the groggy champion back into the ring where he went on to destroy the "Bull of the Pampas." The rule violation was overlooked, for the fight took place at the Polo Grounds in New York. Cortázar never forgot the fight, or its repercussions in Argentina: "quince millones de argentinos retorciéndose en diversas posturas y pidiendo entre otras cosas la ruptura de relaciones, la declaración de guerra y el incendio de la embajada de los Estados Unidos. Fue nuestra noche triste; yo, con mis nueve años, lloré abrazado a mi tío y a varios vecinos ultrajados en su fibra patria" (fifteen million Argentines writhing in various positions and asking for, among other things, the breaking off of relations, the declaration of war, and the burning of the United States embassy. It was our blackest night; I, with all of my nine years, wept in the arms of my uncle and several neighbors whose patriotic pride had been outraged [*Vuelta al día* 2:128]). In the same essay, he recalls how one rainy night in Paris, in 1952, he remembered the great fighters—Gene Tunney, Tony Canzoneri, the Argentines Julio Mocoroa and Justo Suárez, and, greatest of all, Sugar Ray Robinson—and how that reverie produced the story "Torito." In light of this affection for the sport, it is hardly surprising that the three boxing stories are arguably the best of the realistic group.

Torito himself is a former prizefighter, now hospitalized, perhaps punch-drunk, who recounts his career to an old friend. He reflects on his greatest fights: how he laughed at Tani after defeating him, how he destroyed a black fighter named Flores, but especially how he himself was badly beaten by a man he calls simply "el rubio" (the blonde). He sees the irony in his current predicament, lying flat on his back in a hospital, clearly: "Ahí tenés otra cosa que no sé hacer, mirar p'arriba. Todos dijeron que me hubiera convenido, que

hice la gran macana de levantarme a los dos segundos. . . . Tienen razón, si
me quedo hasta las ocho no me agarra tan mal el rubio" (There you have another thing I don't know how to do, look up. Everybody said it would have
been better for me, that I blew it when I got up after two seconds. . . . They
are right, if I stay down until eight, the blonde doesn't take it to me so bad
[*Relatos* 2:276]).

Cortázar's love for his main character is unmistakable, and his affection for
the sport is clearly reflected in his use of language:

Flor de leñada, viejo, se me agachaba hasta el suelo y de abajo me zampaba cada piña
que te la debo. Y yo meta a la cara, te juro que a la mitad ya estábamos con bronca y
dale nomás. Esa vez no sentí nada, el patrón me agarraba la cabeza y decía pibe no te
abrás tanto, dale abajo, pibe, guarda la derecha. Yo le oía todo pero después salíamos
y meta biaba los dos, y hasta el final que no podíamos más, fue algo grande. Vos
sabés que esa noche después de la pelea nos juntamos en un bodegón, estaba toda la
barra y fue lindo verlo al pibe que se reía, y me dijo qué fenómeno, che, cómo fajás, y
yo le dije te gané pero para mí que la empatamos, y todos brindaban y era un lío que
no te puedo contar.

(It was a war, old man, I was in a full crouch and from underneath I was darting in
and out, punch for punch. And I go to the head, I swear that halfway through we
were already teeing off on one another without a break. That time I didn't feel a
thing, my manager was holding me by the head and saying kid don't leave yourself so
wide open, go to the body, kid, keep your right up. I could hear him but as soon as we
came out we started taking it to each other again, and right to the end when we were
both worn out it was great. You know that night after the fight we got together in a
bar, the whole gang was there and it was beautiful to see how the kid laughed, and he
said to me you're unreal, kid, God you can fight, and I said to him I beat you but as
far as I am concerned it was a draw, and everyone drank to us and it was a madhouse I
can't begin to describe. [282]).

According to Luis Leal, "Torito" is as historically and factually accurate as
"The Pursuer."[5] The title character is modeled after Justo Suárez, his manager was Pepe Lectoure, the black fighter, Flores, was Bruce Flowers, and the
blonde who ended Torito's career was Billy Petrolle. That Cortázar empa-
thized with and identified with Torito is clear, even without his statement
that "I was Justo Suárez for two hours."[6] In fact, as Mercedes Rein has argued, Torito is one of the earliest of Cortázar's works to include a character
who is of interest as a human being, not as a narrative function.[7]

"Segundo viaje" (Second trip),[8] perhaps also inspired by Justo Suárez,[9] is
an even better story, and indeed, one of Cortázar's best. It too is told by a
first-person narrator, although this time he is not the protagonist but a close

friend. The protagonist, Ciclón Molina, was an average club fighter who had nonetheless served as sparring partner for Mario Pradás. Pradás had a stellar career in Argentina, and then went north to the United States to fight for the world championship. After several brilliant tune-up bouts, Mario Pradás was destroyed by the champion, Tony Giardello. His career immediately went into decline, and, after a few bad fights, he died. Ciclón Molina, who idolized Pradás, soon began to show moments of greatness in his fights, and eventually he too went north to fight for the title, and to exact revenge from "Tony Giardello, hijo de puta" (Tony Giardello, that son of a bitch [*Relatos* 2:197]).

The narrator is now an old man telling the story of Ciclón to a much younger individual, as his description of one of Molina's warm-up fights in the United States indicates: "Ciclón lo noqueó en el séptimo, no te hablo del delirio en Buenos Aires, vos eras muy pibe y no te podés acordar" (Ciclón knocked him out in the seventh, I won't even tell you about the delirium in Buenos Aires, you were very young and you cannot remember [203]). He became good friends with the fighter, often meeting him in a bar after a fight to discuss the details of what had occurred in the ring. Eventually, he became the one individual to whom Ciclón would confess his most intimate thoughts. However, just as Ciclón was unable to go north with Mario Pradás, the narrator had to stay behind in Argentina when Molina began his quest for the title.

The scenes in which the narrator and his friends gather around early radio sets to listen to the fights are quite reminiscent of the moment, so vividly painted by Cortázar in "El noble arte," in which his family listened to the Firpo-Dempsey match: "la noche con Giardello, nosotros colgados de la radio, cinco vueltas parejas, la sexta de Mario, la séptima empatada, casi a la salida de la octava la voz del locutor como ahogándose, repitiendo la cuenta de los segundos, gritando que Mario se levantaba, volvía a caer, la nueva cuenta hasta el fin, Mario nocaut, después las fotos que eran como vivir de nuevo tanta desgracia, Mario en su rincón y Giardello poniéndole un guante en la cabeza, el final, te digo, el final de todo eso que habíamos soñado con Mario, desde Mario" (the night of the Giardello fight, we were hanging all over the radio, five even rounds, the sixth to Mario, the seventh a draw, almost at the start of the eighth the voice of the announcer, as if he were drowning, repeating the count of the seconds, screaming that Mario was getting up, was falling again, the new count until the end, Mario knocked out, afterward the pictures that were like living so much misfortune all over again, Mario in his corner and Giardello putting a glove on his head, the end, I tell you, the end of all that we had dreamed with Mario, since Mario [203]).

The same scene was then reenacted by Ciclón and Giardello:

Vos sabés muy bien lo que pasó, para qué te voy a contar, las tres primeras vueltas de Giardello más veloz y técnico que nunca, la cuarta con Ciclón aceptándole la pelea mano a mano y poniéndolo en apuros al final del round, la quinta con todo el estadio de pie y el locutor que no alcanzaba a decir lo que estaba pasando en el centro del ring, imposible seguir el cambio de golpes más que gritando palabras sueltas, y casi en la mitad del round el directo de Giardello, Ciclón desviándose a un lado sin ver llegar el gancho que lo mandó de espaldas por toda la cuenta, la voz del locutor llorando y gritando, el ruido de un vaso estrellándose en la pared antes de que la botella me hiciera pedazos el frente de la radio, Ciclón nocaut, el segundo viaje idéntico al primero, las pastillas para dormir, qué sé yo, las cuatro de la mañana en un banco de alguna plaza. La puta madre, viejo.

(You know perfectly well what happened, why should I tell you, for the first three rounds Giardello quicker and more of a technician than ever, the fourth with Ciclón accepting the fight toe to toe and getting him in trouble at the end of the round, the fifth with everyone in the stadium on their feet and the announcer unable to say what was happening in the center of the ring, impossible to follow the exchange of punches other than to scream unconnected words, and almost halfway through the round the straight punch from Giardello, Ciclón slipping to the side without seeing the hook that put him on his back for the full count, the voice of the announcer crying and screaming, the noise of the glass shattering against the wall just before the bottle smashed the front of my radio, Ciclón knocked out, the second trip identical to the first, sleeping pills, what can I say, four in the morning on a bench in some park. Son of a fucking bitch, old buddy. [203–4]).

Unfortunately, this time things ended even more badly than with Firpo or Pradás: Ciclón Molina died the same night of the fight, from the effects of Giardello's devastating hook. Now his friend repeats his story over a drink in a bar, and tries to understand.

"La noche de Mantequilla" ("Butterball's Night")[10] contains a double plot: an account of an actual world-title fight between middleweight Carlos Monzón, the Argentine champion, and José "Mantequilla" Nápoles, the Mexican challenger who also reigned as welterweight champion for many years, a bout that took place in Paris, and the story of a fictitious spectator who is involved in a dangerous political intrigue. The protagonist of the fictitious account, Estévez, is sent by Peralta to the fight to slip a packet of money and papers into the satchel of Walter, a man he does not know. Peralta's plan seems flawless, for surely no one will notice the subtle exchange that is to take place at the height of the championship action.

As in the other stories, Cortázar provides a marvelous description of the fight. Estévez accomplishes his mission without a hitch, but as he is leaving the arena he encounters Peralta and an associate. They drive him away and interrupt his enthusiastic account of the fight and the success of his errand with the news that the man with the satchel was not Walter. Walter had been seized by "them" and tortured until he revealed the entire plan. Peralta had been unable to reach Estévez in time to stop the transfer of papers. As Estévez speculates aloud on how to escape and save his wife and child, it dawns on him that he is like "Mantequilla" who lost the fight on a technical knockout when his corner threw in the towel. A live Estévez, who might be caught and broken by the enemy, is too much of a threat to Peralta, who takes out his pistol to remove that danger.

"Butterball's Night" is clearly a political story, but it is superior to many of Cortázar's "committed" works. The ending is a definite surprise, prepared by the author's astute withholding of information throughout the story and by his diversion of the reader's attention. The reader, like Estévez, becomes totally engrossed in the fight. Against the backdrop of an event that captured world attention and in which a great deal of nationalistic pride was at stake, a political activist (indeed two, counting Walter) loses his life on a remote country road, killed by members of the same cause he supports.

Cortázar was first inspired to write realistic stories on political themes by the Cuban revolution, which finally ousted Batista in 1959, and his style in the early political stories was undoubtedly influenced by Cuban writers. Although his first such work, "Los amigos," is weak, his second, "Reunión" ("Meeting"),[11] is excellent, and considered by some to be one of the author's masterpieces.[12] The story resulted from debates Cortázar had with young Cuban revolutionaries, particularly members of the "Caimán Barbudo" (Bearded Crocodile) group, about what sort of things he should be writing: "it was going to be a friendly challenge that I wanted to make to them. An effort to show them that one can write a fantastic story—that is perhaps the most fantastic in the book—that has, at the same time, revolutionary content."[13] The piece was published in the group's journal, but none of them ever commented on it.

If the story is indeed fantastic, it is only so through Cortázar's exuberant eyes. The events are real, even though they may still seem impossible thirty years later. In late November 1956, a dilapidated yacht, the *Granma*, left Mexico with eighty-two men on board. This group was the nucleus of the Cuban revolution, including Fidel Castro, his brother Raúl, Ernesto "Che"

Guevara, and many other heroes of the revolution. They landed in Cuba in
the wrong spot, in a swamp, and under adverse conditions. Apparently they
were betrayed by one of their own, for Fulgencio Batista's fighter planes and
soldiers descended to eradicate them. A few days later, only fifteen were still
together, yet two years later they swept triumphantly into Havana. "Meeting"
tells the story of the first few days after the landing.

The narrator, only thinly disguised, is Che Guevara, an asthmatic Argentine doctor turned revolutionary. The landing groups have been scattered by
the swamp and by the strafing airplanes, but are trying to make their way to
the Sierra where they will reunite (hence the original title, "Reunion"). Surrounded by wounded and dead companions, and covered with blood and
vomit, the protagonist thinks of his friend Luis (Fidel Castro) and remembers
Mozart's "The Hunt." Eventually, against impossible odds, the men meet
atop a hill. They crack jokes as always, although none of them expected ever
to see the others again.

Within its own context, "Meeting" is highly realistic, with a wealth of de-
scriptive detail that one does not expect from Cortázar. Many of the events
and even the quotes are taken from Che Guevara's account of those dark
days, as is the epigraph for the story. The following account, from Guevara's
description of the intense battle during which he was wounded, is illustrative:
"Alguien, de rodillas, gritaba que había que rendirse y se oyó atrás una voz,
que después supe pertenecía a Camilo Cienfuegos, gritando: 'Aquí no se
rinde nadie . . .' y una palabrota después" ("Someone, on his knees, was
screaming that we had to surrender and then a voice, that I later learned be-
longed to Camilo Cienfuegos, shouting: 'No one surrenders here . . .' followed by a curse."[14] In Cortázar, this passage becomes "sobre todo me
acuerdo de ese que se puso a gritar que había que rendirse, y de la voz que le
contestó entre dos ráfagas de Thompson, la voz del Teniente, un bramido por
encima de los tiros, un: '¡Aquí no se rinde nadie, carajo!'" ("I especially remember that someone began shouting that we had to surrender, and then a
voice that answered him between two bursts of a Thompson gun, the Lieu-
tenant's voice, a roar above the shouting, a: 'No, fuck it, nobody surrenders
here!'" [Relatos 3:115; All Fires 61].

It would be a mistake, however, to assume that Cortázar blindly followed
Guevara's description of what happened. Instead he selected a number of
events that he evidently found particularly significant in Guevara's lengthy
account of the days of the Sierra Maestra and molded them into a fine story.
The narrator's combined recollections of Luis and the music of Mozart gives
the text a poetic quality that is unusual in literature of this type. While the
thinly-disguised Fidel Castro is perhaps overly idealized, he is still a flesh-

and-blood human being, unlike the idol portrayed in many Cuban writings on the same subject. While Alfred Mac Adam is correct in his assessment that "Meeting" is an example of "compromised" literature,[15] it is certainly much more than that, for it is also a highly successful work of art. Moreover, as Néstor García Canclini has pointed out, in this story friendship and brotherhood, just as poetry and jazz do elsewhere, provide the antidote to nihilism.[16]

Cuba and her revolution also provide the backdrop for the much less satisfying "Alguien que anda por ahí" ("Someone Walking Around").[17] In this story, Jiménez, a counterrevolutionary, comes to Santiago to plant a bomb in a factory. He is dropped off by an electric launch and makes his way to a motel where he is met by a coconspirator, Alfonso. During the night he suddenly awakens to find a stranger, a man he previously noticed in the bar, in his room. The stranger says he is simply "someone walking around" who used to be an exile himself (presumably before the revolution). The stranger then chokes Jiménez to death.

While "Someone Walking Around" reflects Cortázar's continuing dedication to political commitment, it fails aesthetically. Its fatal flaw is that the controlling perspective is that of Jiménez, the counterrevolutionary. As he sneaks ashore and into the motel, as he plans his moves and glances furtively about for signs of danger, the tension builds quickly and effectively. Unfortunately, the reader's empathy for Jiménez also consequently builds. Moreover, in the early pages only subtle references to a bomb that is remote-controlled and to Stevenson's last fight (presumably Cuban heavyweight great Teófilo Stevenson, winner of several Olympic gold medals) reveal that Jiménez is plotting against Castro, not Batista. In keeping with Cortázar's political sympathies, the stranger should be the story's hero, but he appears only at the end, when he murders the man with whom the reader identifies.

Other stories, with a more generalized political backdrop, are more successful. After the military junta began the terror of the "desaparecidos" (the disappeared) in his native Argentina in the mid-1970s, Cortázar could find his political material much closer to home. In fact, "Segunda vez" ("Second Time Around")[18] and "Apocalipsis en Solentiname" ("Apocalypse at Solentiname") were both suppressed by the junta's censors in the Argentine edition of *Alguien que anda por ahí.*[19]

"Second Time Around" tells the story of a seemingly innocent woman, María Elena, who is summoned one day by a government agency. The location and external appearance of the building strike her as strange for government offices, but when she enters the designated room, she finds a small group waiting in the outer office. All but one are like herself, responding to the first summons. She strikes up a friendship with the second-timer, a young man named Carlos, who is the last, other than María Elena, to be called into the inner office. When her turn finally comes, she is surprised to notice that the inner offices have no exit other than the one through which she entered, and yet Carlos is nowhere to be seen. After she has completed her interview and received a summons to return for a second time, she waits for Carlos, who never reappears.

This account, narrated from the perspective of María Elena, although not in the first person, is framed by a narrator who obviously is one of the office workers: "No más que los esperábamos, cada uno tenía su fecha y su hora. . . . Ellos, claro, no podían saber que los estábamos esperando" ("We just waited for them, each one had his date and his time. . . . They, of course, had no way of knowing that we were waiting for them" [*Relatos* 4:19; *We Love Glenda* 199]). This narrative frame, which vanishes when María Elena first enters the story, but reappears when she decides to go on without Carlos, makes it clear that those who are summoned back for a "second time around" will "disappear," perhaps forever, and that María Elena will at last find out what happened to her friend: "Capaz que entonces las cosas cambiaban y que la hacían salir por otro lado aunque no supiera por dónde ni por qué. Ella no, claro, pero nosotros sí lo sabíamos, nosotros la estaríamos esperando a ella y a los otros" ("Maybe things would be different then and they would have her go out through the other side, although she didn't know where or why. Not her, no, of course, but us, yes, we knew, and we'd be waiting for her and the others" [26; 207]). Unlike the case in "Someone Walking Around," this change in perspective allows the reader the wider frame necessary to understand what María Elena does not grasp, while still narrating the bulk of the story from her perspective, thus ensuring reader sympathy. The callous indifference of the framing narrator, who is concerned primarily with smoking, coffee, and the horse races, heightens the effect.

Cortázar continued experimenting with perspective in his subsequent collection, including the story "Grafitti" ("Graffiti"), another story of urban political violence.[20] This piece, like "Second Time Around," was based on the mood in Argentina during the military dictatorship that began in 1975.[21] At first the identity of the narrator is unclear, for everything is told in second person: "Tantas cosas que empiezan y acaso acaban como un juego, supongo que te hizo gracia encontrar el dibujo al lado del tuyo" ("So many things begin and perhaps end as a game, I suppose that it amused you to find the sketch beside yours" [*Relatos* 4:7; *We Love Glenda* 33]).

The anonymous narrator continues to tell the story of the also unknown "tú" and his drawings, illegal graffiti sketched hastily on city walls to communicate the anguish of a city imprisoned by its own government. An unknown individual that "tú" recognizes as a woman through her work begins to paint sketches alongside his, thus forming a sort of dialogue through drawings. The graffiti incense the police, who step up their efforts to eradicate both the sketches and those who create them. After a particularly bold and dangerous drawing by "tú," he sees his correspondent arrested and beaten when she tries to answer. The walls of the neighborhood remain clean for days, but eventually "tú" again begins his clandestine activity, now painting the screams of the government's victims.

One night, a picture of a face, smashed and with one eyeball hanging from its socket, is drawn next to his sketch. The final sentences reveal that the narrator is the woman correspondent, who has finally been released by the government, although now completely broken: "¿qué otra cosa hubiera podido dibujarte? ¿Qué mensaje hubiera tenido sentido ahora? De alguna manera tenía que decirte adiós y a la vez pedirte que siguieras. Algo tenía que dejarte antes de volverme a mi refugio donde ya no había ningún espejo" ("what else could I have sketched for you? What message would have made any sense now? In some way I had to say farewell to you and at the same time ask you to continue. I had to leave you something before going back to my refuge where there was no mirror anymore" [11; 38]).

Like Cortázar's other better stories of political commitment, "Graffiti" succeeds because of a poetic and often ambiguous presentation that saves it from the fate of stories that are more specific and declamatory. While there is a certain thematic sameness that unites Cortázar's stories on urban political violence with those of other writers—the endless sirens, unmarked police cars, lorries filled with policemen and soldiers, dry fear and sudden violence—his works are as a whole vastly superior to those of authors who write only to denounce, without acquiring or utilizing the tools of the master storyteller.

The Argentine situation inspired one more short story, "Satarsa."[22] The title derives from a palindrome, "atar a la rata" (tie up the rat), which when attempted in the plural yields "atar a l[as ratas]." Cortázar himself explained the genesis of the story. While he was playing with the word "rata" he thought of the palindrome. Then, "Suddenly the idea of the 'rata' led to a series of ideas by way of the palindrome and those ideas were ideas of horror, ideas that reflected my feelings about the news from Argentina that I had been listening to or reading. Then I began to write palindromes. The story begins, as you know, with a character who does palindromes."[23]

The character in question is Lozano, a refugee from what is apparently a civil strife (according to Alazraki, it is the 1976–83 brutal military repression known as the "guerra sucia").[24] He and his friends capture and sell live rats to sustain themselves and their families, hoping to save enough to be able to move on. Meanwhile they live in abject misery; Lozano's daughter's hand was eaten by rats, and an acquaintance was killed by the giant rodents. Lozano, the bravest and best of the rat hunters, devises a plan to burn hordes of them out of their cave, and capture enough to finance his family's escape to another country. The plan, although extremely risky, seems to work, and after a fierce battle against the rodents Lozano and his companions are on their way home with cages bulging with screaming rats. On the way, however, they are ambushed by a much more ominous pack of "rats," soldiers, who kill all of the refugees.

In some ways, "Satarsa" is a borderline fantastic story, for the vivid accounts of the wars waged against the rats, with men wrapping their legs in leather armor to protect themselves from the swarms of rodents, seem incredible. Moreover, just how, to whom, and why the rats are sold is never made clear. However, the sordid details, the specificity of the violence and degradation, and the interest and sympathy aroused by Lozano, who retains a certain nobility despite his plight, make the story quite realistic. In the fantastic stories, Cortázar tended to avoid this kind of detail, relying instead on powers of indirect suggestion, on events alone, or on phlegmatic remarks by the characters.

The final realistic story, "Recortes de prensa" ("Press Clippings"),[25] again treats the theme of urban violence, but with a radical difference: here it is not institutionalized or perpetrated by the state, or even by an organization, but by individuals, and on a most personal, sordid level. The narrator, Noemí, a famous author living in Paris, is asked by a sculptor, who has done a series of works on the theme of violence, to write a text to accompany his work. While she is studying his sculptures, she shows him a press clipping that is an open letter, written by an Argentine woman living in Mexico, that describes how the woman's daughter and several other members of her family have been tortured and killed by the military junta. Noemí agrees to write the piece. Shortly after she leaves the sculptor's apartment, she finds a small girl crying in the street. The girl tells her that her father is "doing things" to her mother. Noemí follows the girl to a garden shack where she discovers that the father has the mother tied to a bed frame and is burning her with a cigarette. Noemí knocks the man unconscious with a stool and helps his victim tie him in her place. Then Noemí, a sophisticated woman of the world who is repulsed by violence in all its forms, helps torture the man.

The text Noemí writes to accompany the sculptor's work is the story of that evening. He, however, thinks she made it all up, although he finds a coincidence in the newspaper: an account of how a man was tortured to death in the neighborhood where her story takes place. He sends the clipping to her in the belief that she based her piece on that news item. Noemí returns to the area where she encountered the child and finds her again, although she cannot find the building where the torture took place.

"Press Clippings" is perhaps Cortázar's harshest story in terms of its realistic details. It is rendered all the more disturbing by its depiction of how even a cultured author and sworn enemy of violence can suddenly become a torturer. One cannot help but wonder if Cortázar had not come to fear that the monsters he so abhorred and denounced throughout Latin America might dwell within us all, and especially within Julio Cortázar himself.

The realistic stories, on the whole, are less satisfying aesthetically than the other types, although some, particularly those that deal with boxing, are nonetheless excellent. That Cortázar felt that the realistic stories formed a group apart from the others is made clear by his own grouping when he prepared the complete collection: six of the ten are included in the final and briefest volume, "Ahí y ahora" (There and now). The six, "Graffiti," "Second Time Around," "Press Clippings," "Satarsa," "Someone Walking Around," and "Butterball's Night," are joined by only three other works: the gripping portrayal of violence in Nicaragua "Apocalypse at Solentiname," the grim depiction of blindly obedient youths who will serve tomorrow's juntas in "La escuela de noche" (The school by night), and the horrifying view of urban, governmental violence in "Pesadillas" (Nightmares). The content of these nine stories, combined with the ominous volume title "Ahí y ahora," is clearly a warning to the world of what was happening in Latin America.

It is unquestionable that Cortázar eventually felt compelled to subordinate the quality of his art to his message. Having said that, however, one must also admit that the quality of even the most compromised stories is so high as to be envied by many well-known but lesser artists. Those stories that suffer from the weight of their message are few indeed, and many remain that combine seriousness and urgency of content with artistry of the highest imaginable quality.

Chapter Six

The Novels

Although Julio Cortázar's reputation as one of the twentieth century's outstanding authors rests primarily on the number and the quality of his short stories, one of his five novels, *Rayuela* (*Hopscotch*), is more directly responsible for his international fame. Few novels have been so widely translated and read, and fewer still have had such a great literary impact. The other novels vary widely in quality and importance.

For the reader accustomed to the brilliant and precise economy of Cortázar's stories, the novels come as something of a shock, for they tend to be wordy, lengthy, and even ponderous at times. Cortázar believed that "The novel wins by points, while the short story must win by a knockout."[1] Moreover, he once stated that "the novel is a great trunk; it is the possibility of expressing a multitude of contents with enormous freedom, because, in reality, the novel has no rules, except to keep the law of gravity from going into effect and allowing the book to fall from the reader's hands."[2]

While the author did not begin to write short stories until he was in his thirties, he wrote his first novel when he was only nine. A short novel, completed in the late 1940s, was rejected by the publishers for "its nasty words."[3] That work, *El examen* (The exam), which is dated 1950 but was not published until after the author's death,[4] may be the first Cortázar novel to survive, at least in manuscript form.

This work is of little interest except to specialists who are concerned with the full trajectory of Cortázar's development as a writer. It focuses on a brief period in the lives of five characters. Juan and Clara, a young married couple, are to take university exams about twenty-four hours after the novel begins. As they wander about a mysterious, almost surrealistic Buenos Aires, they are accompanied by three friends: Andrés, his girl friend, Stella, and "el cronista" (the chronicler), who works for a newspaper. As the story opens, Clara is impatiently awaiting Juan in the "Casa de Lectores" (House of Readers), a strange educational institution in which professionals read masterworks of world literature aloud for the students. The couple decides not to sleep on the eve of their exam, but to spend the night with their friends.

Juan, Clara, and Andrés are all preoccupied because a certain Abel seems to be shadowing them. Abel's relationship with the others is never made clear, although it is suggested that he was once involved with Clara, and that she had thought him dead. Late in the novel, Clara shows Andrés a letter from Abel that seems to contain threats, thus justifying their concern.[5] Throughout the bulk of the work, however, Abel simply hovers in the background as an ill-defined threat among many other indicators of impending doom.

The novel traces the meanderings of the five friends throughout Buenos Aires as Clara and Juan await the hour of the examination. They visit a mysterious temporary shrine, erected in a tent in the central plaza. The shrine houses bones that are treated as holy relics, before which crowds chant, zombie-like, "ella es buena" (she is good). In addition to this blind, unexplained fanaticism, the city is plagued by strange mushrooms, reportedly unsafe to eat, an oppressive fog of uncertain origin and composition, mysterious fires, explosions, and unexplained and dangerous subsidences that destroy buildings and streets without warning. The sirens of ambulances, police cars, and fire trucks echo throughout the night. Toward dawn, the friends separate and sleep a little. Later in the day, Juan and Clara accompany her father to a concert—a terrible affair reminiscent of the performance described in the short story, "Las ménades" (The bacchantes), during which Clara's father and Juan get involved in an altercation over the use of a public comb. The friends reunite for the examination, but after waiting for several hours, they learn it will not be given. Later, they find the professor in a bar; he blames the dean of the university for not sending a car to take him to the place of the exam.

The five spend the rest of the evening at a bar near the river. A man offers to help them flee the city by boat (just why is never made clear), for a fee. Andrés urges Juan to go and to take Clara with him. After the couple has safely departed, Andrés encounters Abel, who accuses him of helping them to escape. Andrés has a pistol, which he prepares to fire, but the ending is ambiguous, for it seems that Andrés is the one killed. In a final, brief chapter, which takes place the following day, Stella is waiting for Andrés to come home.

Cortázar told Ana Hernández del Castillo that Andrés commits suicide, for he has no reason to live once he has helped his friends to escape, and that his suicide also destroys Abel, who has no independent existence.[6] This explanation is consistent with the suggestion that Andrés and Clara were once lovers (*El examen* 106) but does little to explain the relationship of Abel to the others.

El examen is powerfully, almost bitterly critical of Argentina. It paints a picture of repression, fear, and uncertainty. Education is portrayed in only two lights: in one, students passively listen to books being read aloud; in the other they are exploited and abused victims of indifferent teachers and administrators. Buenos Aires is a nightmare of a city, similar to the fog that envelopes it. The police, and indeed all officials, are to be feared. The lengthy, philosophical dialogues indict even Argentine letters, language, and the intelligentsia: "la inteligencia elige sus zonas y entre ellas no está la Argentina" (the intelligentsia chooses its areas, and Argentina is not among them [39]). Despite its date of composition, the novel contains many parallels to the last days of Perón. Eva Perón died in 1952, and hundreds of thousands thronged to see her body as it lay in state. The pope was petitioned to canonize her, a perpetual flame was placed at her grave, and she was commonly referred to in Argentina as the Madonna of America. The similarity between the throes of fanaticism aroused by Eva's death and those reflected in the novel by the hordes who show their reverence for the bones with their chant "she is good" is uncanny. Moreover, the general social and political decay depicted in *El examen* reflects the Argentine situation shortly before Perón's fall in 1955.

Such social criticism, although present, is much more subdued in *Los premios* (*The Winners*), Cortázar's first published novel.[7] Here, a group of very heterogeneous Argentines embark upon an ocean cruise that they have won in a contest. Among the more interesting characters are: Carlos López, a school teacher; Paula Lavalle, with whom he becomes involved; Raúl Costa, Paula's homosexual friend and traveling companion; Gabriel Medrano, a dentist; Claudia Freire, a recent divorcée with whom Medrano will seek to establish a relationship; Claudia's son, Jorge, and her friend, Persio; Felipe Trejo, a boy of about fifteen who has brought his family along to share in his prize; and, from the lower classes, Atilio Presutti, nicknamed Pelusa.

These and several other winners gather in a restaurant near the docks, from whence they are mysteriously (and in great secrecy) taken to their ship, the *Malcolm*, which is chosen at the very last minute. Shortly after sailing, the *Malcolm* anchors in the middle of the river for several hours. The passengers, particularly the younger and more independent-minded men, become annoyed at being denied access to the ship's stern. When they demand explanations, they are told that an unusual strain of typhus has broken out among the sailors. The passengers are cut off from the sailors and from the radio room, so they are unable to send messages to Buenos Aires. Some of the men, most notably Medrano, López, Costa, and Presutti, try to make it to the stern, unsuccessfully. As their plans continue to develop and be frustrated, Raúl Costa also attempts to seduce the young, athletic Felipe Trejo, and liasons begin to develop between Medrano and Claudia Freire and between

Carlos López and Paula Lavalle. When Claudia's son becomes ill, the rebels, dissatisfied with the doctor's treatment, lock those who oppose them in a room and storm the stern to send a telegram for help. Medrano, the only man to make it to the radio room, is killed, and the voyage thus ends abruptly. The passengers are returned to Buenos Aires by plane and forced to sign documents attesting to the "approved" version of events (Medrano died of the typhus after illegally entering the quarantined area). The rebels, López, Presutti, and Costa, as well as Claudia and Paula, all refuse to sign.

One of the more important aspects of the novel is its portrayal of a broad cross-section of Argentines. Other characters are the pompous Dr. Restelli, like López a teacher, the crippled but arrogant and wealthy Don Galo Porriño, the haughty, social-climbing family of Trejos, the comparatively simple entourage of Presutti, which includes his mother, his betrothed, and her mother, and, also from the lower middle class, Lucio and Nora, an engaged couple.

As Cortázar explained in a note to the Argentine edition (unfortunately excluded from the English version), he was surprised by many of the characters. He expected finer things from Lucio, who turns out to be somewhat cowardly, and whose future with Nora is in doubt once he has succeeded in seducing her, but at the beginning had little sympathy for Alilio Presutti, who became one of the novel's more noble characters. The author was always fond of the novel despite its errors and although he recognized it as a book of innocence.[8] Cortázar began the work while on a long voyage himself, and wrote it as an exploration of character.[9] In fact, as he later pointed out, the voyage itself is far less important than the characters' discovery of themselves.[10]

This development on a human level is paralleled by a more metaphysical exploration that is provided by Persio, whose lengthy and poetic monologues are interspersed throughout the text. Despite the poetic appeal of these somewhat notorious passages, they sometimes become boring, as do the excessive, often overintellectualized dialogues. Cortázar himself seems to have anticipated this criticism, for he has Claudia tell Medrano that when she first began to read novels, she felt the dialogues were ridiculous because they tend to be so uninterrupted (*Premios* 168; *Winners* 144). Moreover, in one of Persio's early monologues, he attacks "bad" readers who would insist on verisimilitude (53; 41).

Despite its defects, *The Winners* is an interesting novel. The development of the characters, who are simultaneously cut off from civilization as they know it yet are forced to mingle and attempt to get along with countrymen from other social circles and classes, is a worthwhile experiment. As

Jorge tells his mother, the passengers are all in a zoo, but they are not the spectators (164; 140). The efforts to reach the stern of the ship, which many critics have read as a metaphysical quest, once successful, provide no answers. The only man to succeed, Medrano, is killed. Jorge recovers from his illness overnight, and the day following the incident, the stern is opened to all passengers. Suddenly what had seemed so important no longer matters; yet one man has been killed and at least one member of the ship's crew has been wounded. As the "winners" fly back to Buenos Aires, "la ciudad los esperaba para cambiarlos, devolverles todo lo que se habían quitado junto con la corbata o la libreta de teléfonos al subir a bordo. Por lo pronto López era nada menos que un profesor" ("the city was waiting to transform them, to turn them all back into what they had been before leaving, along with the necktie and the little black book of telephone numbers. And suddenly Lopez was just a teacher" [422; 370–71]).

Moreover, *The Winners* is significant in that it continues Cortázar's criticism of what he perceived to be the Argentines' blind acceptance of authority and of rigid class divisions. More than half of the passengers (among them all of the older and more established individuals) adamantly oppose any action that might violate the arbitrary rules to which they have been subjected, and all of these characters blame the rebels for the death of Medrano and for the sudden end of the voyage.

Finally, this novel, unlike *El Examen*, initiates, although in a subdued way, the authorial self-consciousness that became typical of Cortázar's later novels: "¿pero todo esto lo piensa Persio, lo piensa Carlos López, quien fabrica estas similitudes y busca, fotógrafo concienzudo, el enfoque favorable? . . . cabe inferir que quizá Carlos López, que quizá Gabriel Medrano, pero sobre todo Carlos López es agente y paciente de estas visiones provocadas y padecidas bajo el cielo azul" ("but is Persio thinking all this, or is it Carlos Lopez? Who is inventing all these similes? Who's looking for the best angle and focus in this conscientious photography? . . . we can conclude that perhaps Carlos Lopez, or Gabriel Medrano, no, I guess Lopez, is both originator and victim of these visions, brought about and undergone beneath the blue sky" [265–66; 232–33]).

Narrative self-consciousness is particularly evident in *Rayuela* (*Hopscotch*), Cortázar's best-known single work. This, the author's second novel to be published, may well have had more of an impact on Spanish American literary history than any other novel of the so-called boom, including Gabriel García Márquez's *Cien años de soledad* (*One Hundred Years of Solitude*).[11] First published in 1963,[12] *Hopscotch* quickly became a best-seller in many languages, and has received more critical attention than any of Cortázar's other works. Much of the novel's success is no doubt due to its timely publication, for it appeared at a time when many individuals, particularly the young, were challenging all aspects of society and its institutions. The war in Vietnam, hippies, Black Panthers, student protests in the United States, France, Mexico, and elsewhere—all are indices of the unrest that marked the period. *Hopscotch*, in many ways, reflects the dissatisfaction of the time, and the search, no matter how futile, for something better. Nonetheless, the book is not limited to a narrow historical period in its appeal, for it continues to be one of the most widely read and discussed works of our time, and its influence on later literature is undeniable.

Nowhere is the novel's iconoclasm more evident than in its structure. The reader is "invited" to follow one of two possible orders. He or she may choose to read traditionally, and linearly, from the first chapter through the fifty-sixth, ignoring the ninety-nine chapters that follow, or may follow the guide provided at the beginning, starting with chapter 73, and skipping from chapter to chapter as directed, until the work has been completely read. The latter method, which jumps from chapter 73 to chapter 1, then 2, 116, 3, 84, 4, 71, and so on, is the only reading that makes sense, for the "traditional" novel is quite incomplete and unsatisfying. Readers who take that option will wonder why so much is made of the work. It is also a mistake to read the work twice, if one begins with the linear reading, for the first fifty-six chapters take on much richer significance when interspersed with the others, following Cortázar's instructions.

Beyond this unusual organization (and, it should be noted, the skipping about is an important part of the aesthetic experience of reading the novel), the work is divided into three principle parts: "Del lado de allá" ("From the Other Side"), which takes place in Paris; "Del lado de acá" ("From This Side"), which takes place in Buenos Aires; and "De otros lados" ("From Diverse Sides"), which contains what are labeled as "capítulos prescindibles" (expendable chapters). These "unnecessary" chapters include fragments taken from newspapers and books, scraps of literary theory, and other miscellany that prove to be quite important when the work is read "hopscotch" fashion, for they provide significant commentary (often through ironic juxtapositions) on what is happening in the more traditional plot line of the novel.

Because of the novel's peculiar structure, critics have dedicated a good deal of attention to its composition and to its place in the Cortázar canon. At first glance, the work might seem to have little to do with the perfectly structured, tightly knit plots of the author's short stories, but, as many critics have observed, the relationship is actually quite strong. Cortázar himself called *Hopscotch* the "philosophy" of his stories, an attitude that is vigor-

ously defended by Jaime Alazraki, who argues that the same impulses that
produced fantastic solutions in the stories lead to existential explorations in
the novels, particularly in *Hopscotch*.[13] This work is particularly close to the
story "El perseguidor" ("The Pursuer"), a piece that the author considered a
miniature *Hopscotch* and a necessary prelude to the longer work.

The protagonist of *Hopscotch*, Horacio Oliveira, does indeed evoke memories of Johnny in the short story. Although he is not gifted with Johnny's gen-
ius for music, he searches day and night for some unknown element that he
senses is missing in his life. Adrift in Paris, he spends much of his time playing
intellectual mind games with a small circle of friends, listening to records
(jazz and classical), smoking, drinking, and wandering the streets. His female
companion, La Maga (The Magician), perceived by herself and by the others
as their intellectual inferior, is nonetheless much more attuned to her sur-
roundings and to life. She is intuitive and straightforward, with neither need
nor capacity for the others' hyperintellectualization. Moreover, La Maga is totally devoted to Oliveira. But he, despite his own relationships with other
women, is wildly jealous, and eventually abandons La Maga because he suspects she has had or may have in the future an affair with Ossip Gregorovius,
one of the members of their group of friends, or "the club" as they call it.

Oliveira leaves La Maga shortly after the death of her infant son,
Rocamodour, and although he soon repents and searches the streets of Paris
for her, he will never find her again. Friends suggest she has gone to nurse
Pola, a former lover of Oliveira who now suffers from breast cancer. Later,
Oliveira looks for her in her native Uruguay, and occasionally exposes his fear
that she committed suicide by drowning, but that fear is never given a factual
basis. The end of Oliveira's relationship with La Maga also brings to a close
the first section of the novel, "Del lado de allá" ("From the Other Side").

"Del lado de acá" ("From This Side") opens with Oliveira back in Buenos
Aires, living with a former girlfriend, Gekrepten, across a narrow street from
one of his oldest friends, Traveler, and his wife, Talita. Oliveira's search is now
much more desperate, for as Saúl Sosnowski has pointed out, his need to ra-
tionalize and intellectualize everything has now cost him what could have
brought him happiness (La Maga).[14] Traveler gets Oliveira a job at the circus
where he and Talita work, but Oliveira's presence puts a strain on his friends'
marriage, for he begins to see in Talita a replacement for, if not a reincarnation of, La Maga. When the circus is sold and the owner purchases an asylum
for the insane, the three friends take up residence there as caretakers, leaving
Gekrepten behind, much to her distress. Oliveira confuses Talita with La
Maga more and more, but recognizes that he is infringing on Traveler's
world. This recognition brings him to fear that Traveler will kill him. Eventu-

ally, he barricades himself in his room, constructing a series of traps made of yarn, basins filled with water and placed strategically on the floor, and other objects placed to warn and protect him from Traveler's approach.

In the climactic scene, Traveler forces his way into the room, where Oliveira is now precariously perched on the window sill. Traveler does all he can to calm his friend and to keep him from jumping from the window. Traveler then retreats to the courtyard below, where he joins Talita, standing on a hopscotch drawing, and looking up at Oliveira, still at the window:

Era así, la armonía duraba increíblemente, no había palabras para contestar a la bondad de esos dos ahí abajo, mirándolo y hablándole desde la rayuela, porque Talita estaba parada sin darse cuenta en la casilla tres, y Traveler tenía un pie metido en la seis, de manera que lo único que él podía hacer era mover un poco la mano derecha en un saludo tímido y quedarse mirando a la Maga, a Manú [Traveler], diciéndose que al fin y al cabo algún encuentro había, aunque no pudiera durar más que ese instante terriblemente dulce en el que lo mejor sin lugar a dudas hubiera sido inclinarse apenas hacia afuera y dejarse ir, paf se acabó.

(That's the way it was, the harmony lasted incredibly long, there were no words that could answer the goodness of those two down there below, looking at him and talking to him from the hopscotch, because Talita had stopped in square three without realizing it, and Traveler had one foot in six, so that the only thing left to do was to move his right hand a little in a timid salute and stay there looking at La Maga, at Manú [Traveler], telling himself that there was some meeting after all, even though it might only last just for that terribly sweet instant in which the best thing without any doubt would be to lean over just a little bit farther out and let himself go, paff the end. [404; 349])

This paragraph marks the end of the "traditional" reading, but the subsequent eight chapters of the alternate and far richer reading make it clear that Oliveira is now recuperating and being cared for by Gekrepten, Traveler, and Talita. Whether he is recovering from his madness, a fall from the window, or some other accident or illness is never made clear.

For Cortázar, these "unnecessary" chapters "were real, for that could have happened with or without the jump from the window; Oliveira could have even jumped from the window and not killed himself." The author went on to state that Oliveira's fear was real and justified, although he was mistaken in believing Traveler would kill him.[15] The uncertainty of events at the end led many interviewers to question Cortázar about Oliveira's suicide. To some, he replied that he was certain his protagonist did not jump, although it was important to the novel to make the reader figure that out rather than being told,[16] but he told others that he had no idea what happens to Oliveira at the end.[17] While many critics accept the concept of a fully open ending, Ana Hernández del Castillo, who has provided some of the finest interpretations of many of Cortázar's works, rejects it: "Once [Oliviera's] defense system is thoroughly broken . . . he faces three possible destinies: madness, suicide, or symbolic castration through his subjection to the motherly Gekrepten." She further believes that Cortázar's comments on the novel fail to explain why Oliveira, when he is about to jump, is thinking of La Maga, and why the first part is so like André Breton's *Nadja*.[18] Although she rejects the total openness preferred by some critics, Hernández de Castillo's three possibilities are quite faithful to the spirit of the book, and her suggested endings are far more logical and satisfying than those of other scholars.[19] The least satisfying readings, as in the case of the short stories, are those that reduce the ending to only one possibility, the most typical being Oliveira's suicide.

The entirely different endings yielded by the two possible readings suggested by the author highlight the significance of the work's structure and the importance of following the "hopscotch" pattern. As Robert Brody observes in his study guide to the novel, some readers of the first edition evidently felt that Cortázar was trying to get them to read the first fifty-six chapters twice, once linearly and again according to the author's instructions. In subsequent editions, Cortázar made it clear that the reader was to choose only one of the alternatives.[20] Brody also points out that in the second reading, chapter 55 is skipped altogether, but it is repeated verbatim in other chapters from the "expendable" section, so that nothing is missed.[21]

Although Cortázar himself has stated that there is no relationship between the "expendable" chapters and the dramatic action of the novel,[22] even those that do not directly advance the main story, such as those that should be read after chapter 56, serve, in many cases, to comment on the main action, as a few examples clearly demonstrate. In chapter 14, a Chinese member of the "club" in Paris shows the others pictures of a man being dismembered alive (these photographs were published by Georges Bataille in *Les Larmes d'Eros*). He observes that "En China se tenía un concepto distinto del arte" ("In China one has a different conception of art" [70; 54]). The reader, horrified at the backwardness of a culture that might consider torture an art, then must turn to chapter 114, which describes in detail an execution in San Quentin Prison, then proceed to 117 and a fragment from Clarence Darrow's defense of Leopold and Loeb in which the famous lawyer describes how a thirteen-year-old girl and a boy of ten were both executed because they were old enough to know the difference between right and wrong. Such careful intercutting provides a powerful commentary on modern values. Chapter 28, which deals with the death of La Maga's son, Rocamadour, who dies largely from neglect (his mother refuses to hospitalize him, believing she can care for him herself) is followed by an "expendable" chapter, 130, which contains a clipping from the London *Observer* on the threat posed to little boys' penises by zippers, and how children should be carefully supervised when going to the bathroom.

The "expendable" chapters are, then, clearly related to the main action, and indeed they were compiled as the rest of the novel was being written, not added on later.[23] In fact, the structure of *Hopscotch* is far more coherent than many readers originally believed. The action unquestionably moves forward in both sections, Paris and Buenos Aires, although Oliveira's aimlessness is not conducive to progress in the sense of the major conflicts and actions typical of traditional novels, a trait that has often led critics to conclude there is neither action nor plot.[24] Moreover, many critics have analyzed the importance of a structure based on characters and their doubles (Traveler is Oliveira's double, Talita is La Maga's, etc.); Brody has studied a structure based not only on doubles and parallels, but on triads as well (love triangles, tripartite structure, etc.); and in a particularly impressive analysis that won praise from Cortázar, Hernández del Castillo has demonstrated that chapter 41 is the exact inverse of chapter 52 in symbolic terms. A number of scholars have also explored the archtypal significance of many characters, a significance that could not exist without a specific narrative function and structure.

Hopscotch is in many ways a novel of symbols and of "figures," as Genover has pointed out.[25] The figure, in fact, is one of Cortázar's favorite concepts. While this is not the place to explore all of its ramifications in depth, the figure is important to an understanding of his novels, particularly with regard to structure. He viewed figures as sets of related characters or concepts. As such, they are closely related to Erich Auerbach's archetypal figures, for, as Boldy has observed, they repeat concepts, structures, or any of a myriad of possibilities.[26] As Cortázar explained in a letter to Ann Duncan: "When I write, I obey structures, mental or sensory polyhedra of which I have no actual *idea*."[27] The relationships between the characters of "Todos los fuegos el fuego" ("All Fires the Fire") or those of "La noche boca arriba" ("The Night Face Up"), some of which live in the past and others in the present, are examples of such figures, as are the doubles found in *Hopscotch*. Cortázar further explained to Omar Prego that "elements that according to natural law are not related . . . as for example this radiator, this table, and that telephone, in certain processes of intuition (or distraction, in accordance with Zen philosophy) instantaneously relate to one another, create a type of figure that does not have to be material. They can be produced from ideas, sentiments, colors."[28]

Figures, then, become an important unifying, structuring element in many of Cortázar's works, particularly in his novels. As Boldy has pointed out, each novel has a force and a counterforce, manifested through the doubles, the figures (structural relationships between episodes, sets of characters, repetitions of texts, etc.), and through the use of double texts.[29] The members of the "club" in Paris are balanced by the members of the circus (later the asylum) in Buenos Aires. *The Winners* offers a double text with the narration of events interspersed with the monologues of Persio. In *Hopscotch*, in chapter 34, Oliveira reads a novel left behind by La Maga. The odd-numbered lines are from the novel he is reading, while the even lines give his thoughts while reading. Isolated episodes in many instances become representative of the entire plot structure.

While these and other relationships are clearly visible to the reader, they became obvious to the author only after the work was finished: "I had no idea of that existence of the double in the novel. It is true that, near the end of the book, Oliviera calls Traveler his doppelgänger, that he feels there is a type of repetition: I accept that. But what I completely failed to realize—and then the readers and critics came along to point it out to me—is that in the figure of Talita I was repeating La Maga."[30]

Cortázar's intuitive, subconscious sense of unity and of figures rescues *Hopscotch* from being what many early readers perceived as chaos. His lengthy description of its process of composition in his interview with Omar Prego reveals how the novel came about, and helps explain its coherence. He was unable to recall precisely when he began to write, but he remembered a particularly hot day in Buenos Aires (the summer heat is a constant presence in the sections that take place in that city) when he saw some individuals, four stories above the street, trying to pass some *mate* and some nails from one window to another across the street.[31] That incident became one of the most famous episodes of *Hopscotch*, chapter 41, in which Talita is persuaded by Oliveira and Traveler to crawl out onto a precarious bridge of planks to give Oliveira a small bag of *mate* and nails. When he wrote this chapter, he foresaw Talita, Traveler, and Oliveira as no more than friends, but after he had written the first section, which takes place in Paris, he saw the need to expand their relationship.[32]

This episode, its revision and final incorporation into the novel, is typical of the composition of the entire work. Some of the Buenos Aires chapters were written in that city. After 1951 Cortázar continued writing and collecting fragments in Paris. Between fragments, as many as five or six years might elapse.[33] *Hopscotch*, then, was not a carefully planned novel, but "a sort of central point to which outlines of heterogeneous things that responded to my experiences at that time in Paris, when I began to occupy myself with the book in depth, gradually adhered, added, stuck, accumulated."[34] Eventually, a book was born:

In reality, *Hopscotch* is a book whose composition responded to no plan. It is a book that has been dissected by the critics—first part, second part, third part, the expendable chapters—and analyzed with great care, but all this with final structures. Only when I had all the papers of *Hopscotch* on a table, that is to say, all that enormous quantity of chapters and fragments, did I feel the need to put it in relative order. But that order was never within me before and during the writing of *Hopscotch*.[35]

In short, the aimlessness one senses in Horacio Oliveira, the novel's protagonist, was present in the author throughout the process of composition. This lack of direction, this sense of only vaguely perceived purpose, has made the novel a favorite for those interested in existentialist philosophy. Oliveira's ill-defined quest is in many ways a search for authenticity, just as Morelli, a fictitious writer who plays an important role in the work, especially in the "expendable" chapters, seeks authenticity of expression.[36] Genover's study of *Hopscotch* as an existential novel highlights the fact that the work marks an important step away from existential pessimism, however, and Garfield aptly points out that Oliveira is not the resigned, passive sufferer typical of many existentialist works. On the contrary, he seeks to transpose his reality through wit, imagination, and a particularly lively sense of humor, all characteristics one does not associate with traditional existentialism.[37]

In part, Oliveira's search is for a sense of center, a point that he only occasionally and vaguely perceives. He frequently gazes into the heavens through the hole in the top of the circus tent, imagines a perfect point at which meaningless lines converge with the eyes of the perceiver to yield a painting (98; 79), and constantly wonders where the "center" might be found: "También este matecito podría indicarme un centro. . . . Y ese centro que no sé lo que es, ¿no vale como expresión topográfica de una unidad? Ando por una enorme pieza con piso de baldosas y una de esas baldosas es el punto exacto en que debería pararme para que todo se ordenara en su justa perspectiva" ("This *mate* might show me where the center is. . . . And just what is this center that I don't know what it really is; can it be the coordinates of some unity? I'm walking back and forth in an apartment whose floor is tiled with flat stones and one of these stones is the exact spot where I ought to stop so that everything would come into its proper focus" [98; 78–79]).

Oliveira never finds the center he seeks; at the end his path seems as labyrinthine as ever. Cortázar originally planned to title the novel *Mandala*, which in Buddhism is a labyrinth that is shaped much like a hopscotch chart.[38] The Argentine version of hopscotch has particular importance to an understanding of the game's symbolism in this work. The diagram resembles a stack of boxes of irregular size, capped off by a domed compartment labeled "heaven." The lowest level is correspondingly named "hell." This diagram becomes particularly significant to Oliveira once he is working in the asylum, for there is a hopscotch chart in the courtyard, beneath his window. It is when Talita plays the game that he most clearly perceives her resemblance to La Maga, and his own, symbolic search for "heaven" is frustrated. In fact, near the end of the novel, he descends into "hell" (the asylum's morgue) with Talita, kisses her, and activates the paranoia that will lead him to barricade himself in his room and threaten suicide.

Despite its playfulness, *Hopscotch* is clearly a most serious book. Moreover, despite its complexity, it is a very readable one. Readers tend to enjoy the challenge offered by the text and the need for them to participate actively in the story-telling, whether through jumping back and forth, from chapter to chapter, or recognizing obscure references and relationships. In the literary discussions included in the novel, centered normally on the works and ideas of Morelli, Cortázar suggests the need to abandon the "lector hembra" (the female reader), a choice of words that would come to haunt him and for which he repeatedly apologized. What he wished to say was that authors must forge ahead into new territory, leaving behind those passive readers who wish to be led by the hand, but gaining readers who enjoy the intellectual challenge of difficult books. The linear reading suggested for chapters 1 through 56 is an offering to the passive readers, while the more meaningful alternate reading is for the type of new reader that Cortázar wished to challenge.

Not all critics have responded favorably, however. Brody, for example, praises the novel's dynamism, but dislikes the stress placed on extraliterary effects.[39] Many have criticized the work for its hyperintellectuality, a characteristic that the author admits pervades his work, but adds, "I'm not willing or able to renounce that intellectuality."[40]

Indeed, it is all the more acute in his next novel, *62. modelo para armar* (*62: A Model Kit*). While Juan Carlos Curutchet's observation that "critics have agreed with rare unanimity in denouncing the monotony, the ponderosity of the first thirty pages—to be more exact, up to the conclusion of Juan's poem"[41] is something of an exaggeration, Stephen Boldy is probably correct in his belief that these same pages have discouraged many readers.[42] The opening section is extremely important, however, for not only does it present the central character, Juan, but it also introduces and begins to intertwine many of the dominant motifs.

On a Christmas Eve in Paris, Juan has taken refuge in the Polidor restaurant, where he is passing the time thumbing through a just-purchased book by Butor and drinking Sylvaner wine. He is seated facing a large mirror, in which he can observe what is going on in the restaurant. The mirror, the book, the wine, and several other elements combined purely by chance at this moment in time lead Juan to reflect on a number of ideas and recent events. The rest of the book illustrates how these seemingly disparate motifs relate to one another.

62 was intended to be radically experimental from the outset. The idea, and the title, come from chapter 62 of *Hopscotch*, in which Morelli envisioned a novel devoid of the traditional rules of psychology. As Cortázar later explained, the characters are motivated by hidden, unexplainable forces, rather than the usual psychological forces employed in most novels.[43] Time, in any rigid sense, and even space are constantly violated. However, if the reader heeds the initial warning and reads without trying to establish plot lines or clear causal connections, the work is far more enjoyable than frustrating:

No serán pocos los lectores que advertirán aquí diversas transgresiones a la convención literaria. Para no citar más que algunos ejemplos, los personajes argentinos pasan del voseo al tuteo cada vez que le conviene al diálogo; un londinense que tomaba sus primeras lecciones de francés se pone a hablarlo con sorprendente soltura (para peor en la versión española) apenas ha cruzado el canal de la Mancha; la geografía, el orden de las estaciones del subterráneo, la libertad, la psicología, las muñecas y el tiempo dejan evidentemente de ser lo que eran bajo el reino de Cynara.

A los posibles sorprendidos les señalo que, desde el terreno en que se cumple este relato, la transgresión cesa de ser tal.

(Not a few readers will notice various transgressions of literary convention here. To give only a few examples: the Argentine characters switch from one familiar form to another whenever it suits the dialogue; a Londoner who is only starting his study of French begins to speak it with amazing fluency (and even worse, in a Spanish version) as soon as he crosses the Channel; geography, the order of subway stations, freedom, psychology, dolls, and time obviously cease being what they were in the realm of Cynara.

For those who might possibly be startled, I pointed out that in the territory where this tale takes place the transgressions cease to be such.)[44]

Narrative perspective constantly shifts, and matters are made even more difficult by the presence of *paredros* and the dominance of "the city."

The term *paredros*, as the author explained, refers to the double of an Egyptian deity, an associated divinity,[45] and is used in the novel to indicate another character with whom a narrating character feels a particular affinity at any given moment. Thus, as the narrative perspective changes, or even as a narrating character's mood or thoughts change, the identity of the character designated by *paredros* is in constant flux, and is often impossible to determine: "cualquiera podía ser el paredro de otro o de todos y el serlo le daba como un calor de comodín en la baraja" ("anyone could be the paredros of another or of all and being it gave him something like the value of a joker in cards" [30; 30]).

Likewise, "the city" is not a fixed place, or even a real one; it exists in the minds of the characters as a dreamlike urban center that all of them have visited at one time or another, and to which many return, although unlike in the real cities where the action takes place—London, Paris, Vienna—in "the city" they have difficulty meeting one another. "The city" is the product of a dream that obsessed the author from his youth, a dream in which he went into an unknown yet well-defined metropolis in search of something or someone. It is described in the poem, apparently written by Juan, that concludes the first segment.

The central characters are: Juan, like Cortázar a translator and the character with whom the author most closely identified;[46] his mistress, Tell; the sculptor, Marrast; his mistress, Nicole; two Argentines, Calac and Polanco, also known as the Tartars, who provide the novel with its comic relief; Hélène, an anesthetist with whom Juan is obsessed and who is herself haunted by the vision of a dead patient who resembled Juan; Celia, a youthful runaway, forcibly seduced by Hélène; and Austin, a young English lutanist and Marrast's student of French. Among the peripheral characters are Feuille Morte, a woman who is apparently retarded, and Monsieur Ochs, an elderly dollmaker who never appears directly, but who has a strong influence on the action.

Given the premises upon which the novel was composed, it is impossible to trace a clear plot outline. For the most part, things simply happen and are presented to the reader through a variety of perspectives. Most of the characters, as in the author's other novels, are restless and dissatisfied with their lives, and, as in previous works, a great deal of time is spent drinking wine, smoking, and discussing. No one is content in his or her current sexual liason: Nicole, living with Marrast, is in love with Juan. Marrast is in love with Tell, Juan's mistress, and Juan is obsessed with Hélène. As Garfield has pointed out, "Desire is always tinged with egoism, sadism, lesbianism [*sic*], idealism or indifference, but rarely with unselfish and sharing love."[47]

However, if one abandons the expectations associated with traditional, linear narratives, as cautioned in the first pages, and allows the characters to coalesce by association, rather than stand as unique and separate individuals, the work takes on a fascinating, kaleidoscopic nature. As the author explained, the group, "connected by love or by friendship, constitutes a type of constellation, of superindividuality, in which the acts that each of the members believes to be a product of free choice are born from a series of voluntary interactions that unleash reactions, limited or in series; destinies are intertwined and set free."[48] This nebulous causality extends far beyond the limits of the group, as Hélène reflects, "somos mucho más la suma de los actos ajenos que la de los propios" ("we're much more the sum of the acts of others than our own" [246; 264]).

The constellations of characters are obviously related to the concept of figures, explored in other works, and here one can see more clearly than ever the author's interest in precipitates and crystallizations as narrative possibilities.[49] The opening scene is again illustrative. Juan, drinking his Sylvaner in the Polidor restaurant, overhears a customer ordering a *château saignant* (7; 7). This "bloody castle" flows into associations of vampirism and the Basilisken Haus on Blutgasse, where a legendary countess once drained the blood of innocent virgins until she herself was walled into a room to die of starvation.[50] A peripheral character, Frau Marta, is assumed by Juan and Tell to be a modern-day vampire, a reincarnation of the countess. Later Hélène coalesces with these figures: the novel contains frequent images of her standing over the nude, bloodless body of the patient who reminds her of Juan; Juan's throat is sore after he and Hélène make love; Hélène seduces the young virgin, Celia; Austin, seeking revenge for Celia, kills Hélène by stabbing her in the heart. Throughout the novel, literary motifs, legends, characters, ideas, etc., flow together in this manner.

These conglomerate images also give the work a much stronger sense of cause and effect than one might expect. While the novel has clear affiliations with the French *nouveau roman*, Cortázar clearly achieved his goal of writing a work that collected such images into a narrative with a strong complication and denouement.[51] Hélène's death, although unexpected, is obviously the result of earlier actions, and the dissolution of the group at the end seems a logical result of previous conversations and events.

In fact, many of the novel's finer sequences depend heavily on traditional ingredients of cause and effect. Marrast, for example, publishes an unsigned letter to the members of an organization called Neurotics Anonymous, urging them to solve "el enigma del tallo" ("the enigma of the branch" [44; 48]) that is portrayed in a painting in a museum in London. He and other members of the group then gather to observe the neurotics crowding around the previously ignored painting. The popularity of the painting becomes so great that nervous museum officials remove it and store it in a vault. One member of Neurotics Anonymous, Austin, is incorporated into the group of friends, becomes Marrast's pupil, falls in love with Celia, and ultimately murders Hélène.

Chance, coincidence, and surprise nonetheless characterize much of the action. Monsieur Ochs, for example, a sixty-year-old dollmaker, hides within each of his dolls a surprise that can be discovered only when the doll is broken. In some he places money, in others an obscene object (apparently a phallus), that scandalizes the mothers of the girls who own the dolls, and nothing in still others. When word gets out, many mothers destroy their children's dolls hoping to find money. Those who find phalluses complain to the authorities, and Ochs is finally prohibited from making additional dolls. One, however, finds its way from Juan, to Tell, to Hélène, and is broken by Celia.

The rather perverse humor exemplified by Marrast and Ochs gives way to slapstick in the case of the Argentines, Calac and Polanco. These two middle-aged men, Calac, a writer, and Polanco, an experimenter who fancies himself a scientist, live together like a quarrelsome old couple. In one episode, Polanco attaches the motor from a lawn mower to a small boat. The maiden voyage strands the two friends and a *paredros*, whose identity is unclear, on a tiny island. Even though they are close enough to those on shore to carry on a normal conversation and the water is but four feet deep, they prepare as if they were to be marooned for months, rationing cigarettes and pooling resources. Calac, who is busily taking notes on the group's conversation during a train ride near the end of the novel, is apparently the author of the entire work, a fact confirmed by Cortázar.[52]

62 is in some respects, then, a mixed success. Although he often despaired of the difficulty of writing a book such as Morelli described in *Hopscotch*, the author was successful in writing a radically experimental novel. He had to abandon, to some degree, the rigidity of Morelli's prescription because the characters threatened to become too robotic.[53] That decision, however, is undoubtedly responsible for making the novel so enjoyable to read. Even so, the work remains extremely complex and difficult and critical reaction has been divided. Although, as Alazraki has argued, it "is built with the precision and cleverness of a clockwork,"[54] it will never challenge the lofty place of *Hopscotch* in the Cortázar canon.

Although critics tend to dislike the complexity of *62*, they also disparage Cortázar's final novel, *El libro de Manuel* (*A Manual for Manuel*),[55] for the clarity and force of its social message. This work, like many of the later short stories, reflects the author's desire to establish a clear literary record of his political views without betraying his determination to create only literature of high quality. In *A Manual for Manuel* an obscure group of revolutionaries, comprised primarily of Latin Americans now living in Paris, carry out an elaborate plan to kidnap a Latin American VIP, the ransom for whom is to be the freedom of a number of political prisoners. The kidnapping is successful, but the *hormigas* (ants), a sort of international police force, trap them, wounding at least one, and perhaps killing another. Only the intervention of the French police prevents the "ants" from killing the kidnap victim and blaming the revolutionaries.

As in the case of 62, the *Manual* contains a number of intertwining stories, many of which deal with personal interrelationships. Unlike the previous work, however, this novel is dominated by two narrative threads. Andrés, an Argentine who is clearly the character closest to Cortázar, is, like Oliveira in *Hopscotch*, an uneasy expatriot who has no clear sense of direction in his life. His relationship with the Polish actress, Ludmilla, is comfortable but insufficient. He prefers jazz records, literature, and art to political action. Consequently, he is left behind when Ludmilla is won over to the cause of the revolutionaries, the actions of whom provide the other principal narrative thread. Andrés's story is one of searching for purpose. Once the kidnapping has finally taken place and he realizes that Ludmilla is with the revolutionaries, he joins them at their precarious hideout, endangering his friends and the success of their plan, thinking that he too can be dedicated to their cause. Later he is one of the compilers of the manuscript, which is to become the novel itself.

The story of revolutionary action, complexly entangled with that of Andrés, is, at first, one of minor disruptions of the domestic Parisian routine. The activists provoke disturbances in crowded movie theaters, create scenes in a number of public places, and sabotage venders by placing packets of used matches and cigarette butts among new, unsold wares. Meanwhile, they are carrying out more serious, elaborate plans: importing counterfeit U.S. dollars from Argentina, all of which are exchanged for francs at precisely the same time but in a number of Parisian banks, and, of course, kidnapping the VIP.

Reader sympathy for the revolutionaries is created, at first, not only by showing the political struggle from within the organization, "La Joda" ("the Screwery"),[56] but also by treating the social disruptions and even the plans for the kidnapping with a good deal of humor. Moreover, the text is interspersed with a large number of clippings from newspapers and other documents, preserved in their original print to emphasize their authenticity, that powerfully reflect the nature and extent of injustice throughout the world. This documentary evidence reflects a wide range of horrors, from the mistreatment suffered by hippies traveling in Central America, through the torture of political prisoners throughout the world, to American atrocities in Vietnam. Everywhere the indictment of dictatorships, particularly those supported by the United States and in which the CIA is actively involved, is strong.

Readers who know Cortázar only through this novel may think him extremely left-wing and rabidly opposed to the United States, an opinion that would be somewhat skewed. As his other writings, and even certain passages of *A Manual for Manuel* clearly indicate, his antagonism toward the United States, and toward any country for that matter, was based on what he perceived to be major injustices for which the country is at least in part to blame. His fear of the most ardent revolutionaries, often expressed in his interviews and essays, is here stated by Andrés, a character who strongly reflects the attitudes of the author:

> Gómez y Roland y Lucien Verneuil son de esos que repetirán la historia, te los ves venir de lejos, jugarán la piel por la revolución, lo darán todo pero cuando llegue el después repetirán las mismas definiciones que acaban en los siete años de cárcel de Bukovsky que por allá algún día se llamará Sánchez o Pereyra, negarán la libertad más profunda, esa que yo llamo burguesamente individual y mea culpa, claro, pero en el fondo es lo mismo, el derecho de escuchar *free jazz* si me da la gana y no hago mal a nadie, la libertad de acostarme con Francine por análogas razones, y tengo miedo, me dan miedo los Gómez y los Lucien Verneuil que son las hormigas del buen lado, los fascistas de la revolución.
>
> (Gómez and Roland and Lucien Verneuil [members of the Screwery] are of those who will repeat history, you can spot them from far off, they'll risk their necks for the revolution, they'll give everything but when the afterwards arrives they'll repeat the same definitions that end up with seven years in jail for Bukovsky who over there someday will be named Sánchez or Pereyra, they'll deny the deepest freedom, the one I bourgeoisly call individual and mea culpa, of course, but underneath it's the same thing, the right to listen to free jazz if I feel like it and I don't hurt anyone, the freedom to go to bed with Francine for analogous reasons, and I'm afraid, I'm afraid of the Gómezes and Lucien Verneuils who are the ants of the good side, the fascists of the revolution. [374; 354]).

As Cortázar told Omar Prego while discussing *A Manual for Manuel* and his personal experience with young revolutionaries in Paris, "I was appalled by their dramatic, tragic sense of action, in which there was not the slightest crack to let in even a smile, and even less a ray of sunshine."[57]

Marcos, one of the most important members of the Screwery, and the character with whom Ludmilla falls in love, is much more sympathetic than Roland, Gómez, and Verneuil, for not only is he equally dedicated to the cause, he is also far more human. His fate is ambiguous, for he never appears after the scene in which the Screwery battles the "ants" at the hideout. Cortázar was pleased by the many interpretations offered by critics,[58] but admitted that the corpse being washed by Lonstein (one of the group of close friends but only marginally involved in the Screwery) was probably that of Marcos.[59]

Despite the strong political content of the novel, it is also: "the defiant assertion of an author who embraces socialist revolution but also warns that he will not sacrifice his personal freedom—his erotic rites, his aesthetic preferences, his imagination and his humor—for any ideology."[60] Indeed, Cortázar's usual playfulness and fondness for complex structure and intellectual games are quite evident.

A constant presence in *A Manual for Manuel* that is particularly disorienting is that of "el que te dije" ("the one I told you"), a character whose identity is never revealed. In some ways, "the one I told you" is more perplexing than the *paredros* of *62*, for while in the earlier work the reader is able to discern that the identity of the *paredros* is in constant flux depending on the narrative perspective and the context, "the one I told you" continuously tempts the reader to identify him with one of the named characters, a seemingly impossible task. Cortázar's remarks suggest that, unlike the *paredros*, "the one I told you" is a constant character,[61] another member of the Screwery, and the corpse near the end may even be his.[62]

In any case, "the one I told you" is largely responsible for the text itself. He constantly takes notes, making careful observations, and apparently has also worked on organizing all of the pieces for the scrapbook that Susana and Patricio, additional members of the Screwery, assemble for their infant son, Manuel (hence the title of the book). In fact, all of the friends, even those not involved directly in political activities, contribute news clippings, advertisements, and other documents for the *Manual*, which is intended, one day, to reveal to the child the world into which he was born. The final preparation of the manuscript is the work of Andrés. This explanation of the work's genesis is, however, misleading, for a substantial amount of material is provided that would be beyond the ken of either character.

This is especially true in the cases of those episodes that involve the personal life of Andrés. He is emotionally torn between his two lovers, Ludmilla and Francine, and often, particularly in his moments of extreme doubt, which almost invariably culminate in erotic lovemaking, the narrative perspective is theirs, not his. Andrés's ideal would be for the two women to share him, but they are already both far more tolerant than he (he keeps each apprised of his relationship with the other), as he discovers when he learns that Ludmilla has fallen in love with Marcos.

Andrés approves of Ludmilla's gradual involvement with the Screwery, although at first he thinks their social disruptions silly and nonproductive, and seems to admire Marcos's dedication to the cause. He himself is without purpose or direction. Nonetheless, his eventual alliance with the Screwery seems more a result of his desire to be with Ludmilla than of any social conversion (365; 345), even though he feels he is experiencing "la muerte de un pequeñoburgués" ("the death of a petit bourgeois" [312; 294]).

His farewell gesture to Francine is to force her to go to a hotel room overlooking a cemetery, frighten her by dragging her, nude, out onto the balcony to view the tombs, and sodomize her. At first she cries, "¿Por qué me estás envileciendo?" ("Why are you debasing me?" [296; 278]), but later she implies that he has in fact debased himself: "No, no me has envilecido—dijo Francine casi sin voz—, pero y tú, Andrés, y tú" ("'No, you didn't debase me,' Francine said, almost in a whisper, 'but what about you, Andrés, what about you'" [348; 328]).

Throughout the novel, Andrés is haunted by a dream in which he is given a mysterious mission, expressed in a brief phrase that he has forgotten. Finally he realizes that the mission is "Despertate" ("Wake Up" [379; 359]), presumably to the world about him. Although he has been excluded from the Screwery's plans, he has revealed what he knows to Francine, an outsider, and further endangers his other friends by joining them after the kidnapping has taken place. He saves Ludmilla from exposing herself to the bullets of the police, and ultimately plays a major role in telling the Screwery's story by preparing the final manuscript.

The complexity of the novel is reflected in the difficulties experienced by "the one I told you" and Andrés in organizing the materials. Most characters have several code names and aliases, and events are so confusing they are nearly impossible for the compilers (and for the reader) to keep straight: "el que te dije ya no controlaba el fichero, que saliera cualquier cosa, qué joder" ("the one I told you was losing control of his notes, let anything come out, what the fuck" [314; 296]). A number of scenes deal with the labor of compiling the manuscript.

Even so, as in other Cortázar novels, the reader who is willing to be swept along by the language will have little difficulty in following the main threads: the activities and plans of the Screwery and the personal story of Andrés. One of the finer sections of the work intertwines several narrative scenes. In one, Lonstein, a consummate masturbator, and "the one I told you" discuss the former's "art" and the latter's difficulties in preparing the manuscript. Another scene portrays the lovemaking of Marcos and Ludmilla, another the lovemaking of Andrés and Francine, and still another the progress of the kidnapping plot.

All in all, *A Manual for Manuel* is a much better novel than critics have recognized. While it achieves the author's goal of making a strong political statement, it accomplishes this goal without making major aesthetic sacrifices. Moreover, it continues Cortázar's assault on social taboos, particularly the erotic. As Boldy points out, "it is a brave and honest book, and is an important experiment within the political fiction which characterizes the seventies."[63]

Hopscotch, however, is clearly Cortázar's most important novel, and is perhaps the only one that will be highly regarded by future literary historians. Even so, *62: A Model Kit* has a great deal of appeal for those who like their novels unusually difficult and complex, and *A Manual for Manuel* offers a rewarding blend of political statement and literary artistry. Many readers will agree with David Gallagher's assessment that "there is alas an alienating modishness in Cortázar's novels, a dogged determination to impress us with the vast range of his reading for instance. . . . Yet his work is redeemed by the sheer anarchic humour that is often deployed in it."[64] Clearly these novels are not for the casual reader, and even many serious literati will find them frustrating. Nevertheless, these three works in particular, *Hopscotch, 62: A Model Kit*, and *A Manual for Manuel*, are far more satisfying than many manifestations of the French *nouveau roman*, a form that Cortázar criticized for its failure to replace the worn-out literary conventions it discarded with "new novelistic elements."[65]

Chapter Seven
Miscellanea

Julio Cortázar published four additional important books, each of which almost defies description. Two, *La vuelta al día en ochenta mundos* (*Around the Day in Eighty Worlds*) and *Ultimo round* (Final round), are collections of miscellany, including essays, poems, short stories, vignettes, photographs, and drawings. The other two, *Historias de cronopios y de famas* (*Cronopios and Famas*) and *Un tal Lucas* (*A Certain Lucas*), are less varied, offering a mixture of fantasy, fiction, and essay.

Cronopios and famas[1] was an important precursor to *Hopscotch*, for here Cortázar declared war on conventionality, using as his primary weapons the illogical and a keen sense of humor.[2] The first section, the "Instruction Manual," immediately attacks quotidian reality:

Meter la cabeza como un toro desganado contra la masa transparente en cuyo centro tomamos café con leche y abrimos el diario para saber lo que ocurrió en cualquiera de los rincones del ladrillo de cristal. Negarse a que el acto delicado de girar el picaporte, ese acto por el cual todo podría transformarse, se cumpla con la fría eficacia de un reflejo cotidiano. Hasta luego, querida. Que te vaya bien.
(Drive the head like a reluctant bull through the transparent mass at the center of which we take a coffee with milk and open the newspaper to find out what has happened in whatever corner of that glass brick. Go ahead, deny up and down that the delicate act of turning the doorknob, that act which may transform everything, is done with the indifferent vigor of a daily reflex. See you later, sweetheart. Have a good day. [9; 3])

Included in this section are instructions on how to cry—"se tapará con decoro el rostro usando ambas manos con la palma hacia dentro. . . . Duración media del llanto, tres minutos" ("cover the face decorously, using both hands, palms inward. . . . Average duration of the cry, three minutes" [11; 6])—how to sing—"Empiece por romper los espejos de su casa" ("Begin by breaking all the mirrors in the house" [12; 7])—how to climb a staircase—"Nadie habrá dejado de observar que con frecuencia el suelo se pliega de manera tal que una parte sube en ángulo recto con el plano del suelo, y luego la parte siguiente se coloca paralela a este plano, para dar paso a una nueva perpendicular, conducta que se repite en espiral o en línea quebrada hasta alturas sumamente variables" ("No one will have failed to observe that frequently the floor bends in such a way that one part rises at a right angle to the plane formed by the floor and then the following section arranges itself parallel to the flatness, so as to provide a step to a new perpendicular, a process which is repeated in a spiral or in a broken line to highly variable elevations" [21; 21])—and how to perform a number of additional tasks that are so common as to be automatic.

Instructions for less usual activities are included as well, such as how to understand three famous painters and how to kill ants in Rome. The English version even has "Instructions on How to Dissect a Ground Owl."[3]

Not only does Cortázar bring to our consciousness the complexity of many everyday tasks—"Para subir una escalera se comienza por levantar esa parte del cuerpo situada a la derecha abajo, envuelta casi siempre en cuero o gamuza, y que salvo excepciones cabe exactamente en el escalón" ("To climb a staircase one begins by lifting that part of the body located below and to the right, usually encased in leather or deerskin, and which, with a few exceptions, fits exactly on the stair" [21; 22])—he also alters our perception of everyday reality. When, for example, someone gives the gift of a watch:

Te regalan la necesidad de darle cuerda todos los días, la obligación de darle cuerda para que siga siendo un reloj; te regalan la obsesión de atender a la hora exacta en las vitrinas de las joyerías, en el anuncio por la radio, en el servicio telefónico. Te regalan el miedo de perderlo, de que te lo roben, de que se te caiga al suelo y se rompa. Te regalan su marca, y la seguridad de que es una marca mejor que las otras, te regalan la tendencia a comparar tu reloj con los demás relojes. No te regalan un reloj, tú eres el regalado, a ti te ofrecen para el cumpleaños del reloj.

(They gift you with the job of having to wind it every day, an obligation to wind it, so that it goes on being a watch; they gift you with the obsession of looking into jewelry-shop windows to check the exact time, check the radio announcer, check the telephone service. They give you the gift of fear, someone will steal it from you, it'll fall on the street and get broken. They give you the gift of your trademark and the assurance that it's a trademark better than the others, they gift you with the impulse to compare your watch with other watches. They aren't giving you a watch, you are the gift, they're giving you yourself for the watch's birthday. [23; 23–24])

The second section, "Ocupaciones raras" ("Unusual Occupations"), contains a series of vignettes about a most peculiar family living on Humboldt Street (the author's old neighborhood) in Buenos Aires. Many of these, because of length, development, and structure, could properly be considered short stories, although they are rarely classified as such, even by the author. The first, "Simulacros" ("Simulacra" 27–31; 29–34), introduces the narrator's large, extended family and some of its peculiar habits. In this case, despite the narrator's assurances that the family lacks originality, they decide to build an executioner's platform, complete with instruments of torture and a gallows, in the yard behind their house. The construction is carefully planned to coincide with the full moon, and the girls in the family practice their howls. The project, once recognized, is most distressing to the neighbors, but because the building site is protected by a strong fence, they are helpless to intervene. When the gallows is finally erected, the family eats supper on the platform, watches the moon rise, and finally goes off to bed. The neighbors seem disappointed, perhaps because they had feared (and eagerly anticipated) that the instruments would actually be put to use.

Other selections about the family are equally playful. When a distant relative becomes a government minister, they arrange to be put in charge of a post office. They freely distribute prizes to patrons: balloons for those who purchase stamps, vodka and an occasional veal cutlet to those sending money to relatives. At the parcel post window, they tar and feather the packages so the string and sealing wax are hidden, and only the address shows through a little window in the feathers. In another piece, members of the family tear out pieces of their hair, tie the bundle in a small knot, and wash it down the sink drain. Then they set about trying to recover that exact piece of hair, pursuing it throughout the plumbing system, even through the city sewers, not giving up until they reach the river.

"Conducta en los velorios" ("Our Demeanor at Wakes" 46–50; 49–54) has, like "Simulcra," the length and structure of a short story. When someone in the neighborhood dies, the Humboldt Street family first determines if the grief displayed by the family of the deceased is genuine or feigned. If it is genuine, the Humboldt Street family stays home, but if it is feigned, the entire clan descends on the wake, taking it over completely. The method is simple: members of the Humboldt Street family position themselves as close to the casket as possible and begin to weep until everyone present can see clearly that they are more grief-stricken than the family of the deceased. This action shames the immediate family into a greater show of mourning. When the funeral cortège departs for the cemetery, the invaders usurp the first cars, often leaving members of the immediate family to catch a bus or a taxi. At the ceremony, they again occupy the seats reserved for closest relatives, and offer lengthy eulogies that totally eclipse the paltry offerings of the immediate relatives—if, indeed, the latter even dare to offer their previously prepared speeches once they have heard the oratory skills of the family from Humboldt Street. Then, the clan steals quietly away, leaving the stunned and thoroughly humiliated mourners to fight with their neighbors over control of the lowering of the coffin.

The third section, "Material plástico" ("Unstable Stuff"), is the least satisfying portion of the book. Here, Cortázar's flights of fancy occasionally become excessively obtuse, although one might argue that Cortázar made them deliberately so as an attack on social norms. Under the title "Maravillosas ocupaciones" ("Marvelous Pursuits" 55–56; 59–60) he includes cutting the leg off a spider and sending it to the Minister of Foreign Affairs, or building a mound of sugar on a table in a restaurant, then spitting on top of the mound so that the saliva slides down like a glacier. One particularly childlike and amusing vignette describes how a bear (the narrator) inhabits the plumbing system of a house, running through all the pipes and flues to keep them clean and in good working order.

The final section, which gives the volume its title, has had the greatest impact because of its delineation of three types of creatures—cronopios, famas, and esperanzas—types that soon became an important part of the vocabulary of Cortázar and his critics. A number of vignettes distinguish sharply between the cronopios and the famas, but the esperanzas are never developed to any recognizable degree. Famas are perfectly organized—when they travel, every detail is attended to, even down to lists of doctors on emergency call in the cities they visit. Cronopios cannot find vacancies in the hotels, their weather is miserable, they miss their trains, and they can find no taxis. Yet cronopios love to travel and are delighted by everything they see. Cronopios are happy, intuitive, instinctive creatures. Famas are logical and organized. Cronopios tend to be artists, while famas make good business leaders. Esperanzas are sedentary. The doors to their homes illustrate some of their differences. An esperanza has a plaque that reads, "Bienvenidos los que llegan a este hogar" ("Welcome all who come to this home"); the fama has no welcoming sign; the cronopio has five. The first four repeat the standard platitudes, "Welcome all who enter here," "The house is small but the heart is immense," "The presence of a guest is as soft as rest," "We are poor but still we have good will." The final plaque, however, reads, "Este cartel anula todos los anteriores. Rajá, perro" ("This placard cancels all of the others. Beat it" [124; 146–47]). Cortázar was proud to be a cronopio, a term he also used to flatter his friends and those he admired. The greatest cronopio of all was Louis Armstrong, whose concert in Paris is described in "Louis enormísimo cronopio" ("Louis, Super-Cronopio") in *Around the Day in Eighty Worlds* [2:13–22; 66–71).

The playfulness that dominates *Cronopios and Famas* is equally evident in *A Certain Lucas*.[4] Lucas would certainly have to be a cronopio. When he goes shopping for matches for a friend, he finds himself entangled in everyone else's problems, stopping to help in each case. In a café he runs into a friend who insists that Lucas help him persuade the pharmacist to dispense medicine for the friend's sister; the pharmacist's wife convinces him to take pictures of her daughter's birthday party; a man is injured in a fall and Lucas climbs into the ambulance with him, but at the hospital has to explain what he is doing there since he is not a relative; he is unable to find a taxi to return home, and gets on a bus going in the wrong direction. As he stands on the opposite end of town, waiting for another bus that he suspects may never come, he is approached by an old lady who needs a match ("Lucas, sus compras" 19–23; "Lucas, His Shopping" 9–13).

For the most part, *Lucas* is a collection of such misadventures. He disrupts concerts and is unceremoniously thrown out. He begins a lecture with an attempt to specify his theme, using the table in front of him in contrast to the world at large as an example of the need to be specific about one's topic, but the table and his comments upon it become the lecture. He goes to great lengths to create a special birthday cake for a friend, but at the party he smashes it into her face, without explanation, and is thrown out into the rainy street. He sends love notes clear across the city by snail messenger so that he can savor the delicious wait. When he is hospitalized and a friend sends him a daisy, he asks the nurses to bring a table to set it on, then suggests that the table needs some chairs for friends, then requests some whiskey for the friends to drink, then asks for a wardrobe to make the room tidier and upon which to place the daisy, since there is no longer room on the table. Finally, when the nurses are finished moving and arranging furniture, Lucas throws the flower away, because he does not care much for daisies anyway.

A Certain Lucas is tripartite, with the first and final sections dealing with the personality and misadventures of the title character, while the second part is unrestricted. The tone is maintained throughout, however, and each section is comprised of a number of short vignettes, sketches, or commentaries. "Love 77," for example, from part 2, describes love, presumably in 1977: "Y después de hacer todo lo que hacen, se levantan, se bañan, se entalcan, se perfuman, se peinan, se visten, y así progresivamente van volviendo a ser lo que no son" ("And after doing everything they do, they get up, they bathe, they powder themselves, they perfume themselves, they comb their hair, they get dressed, and so, progressively, they go about going back to being what they aren't" [115; 87]). Other pieces from this section, although humorous, have an equally serious underlying concern. "Texturologías" ("Texturologies"

95–98; 70–73), for example, parodies the nature of literary polemics. The debate is set off when Michel Pardal writes a review of José Lobizón's collection of poetry, *Goose Grease* (presumably all proper names and titles are invented by Cortázar). Pardal, writing in a French journal, attacks the work as a "poverty-stricken product of Latin American poetry" (95; 70). Another critic, writing in a U.S. journal, attacks Pardal and his lack of understanding of the process of creation, and is in turn denounced, in Russia, for her ideological intentions. A British scholar then takes the Russian critic to task for his primitive approach to criticism, only to be lambasted in turn by a Frenchman, for his ignorance of the work of Saussure. A Mexican scholar then writes a glowing commentary on the work of the Frenchman, and quotes from the poetry collection entitled *Goose Grease* to validate his position. Needless to say, any mention of the original, literary cause of the debate has been missing since the first attack on the initial article. Its reintroduction at the end is quite accidental and ironic.

"Texturologies" is a masterful parody of self-interested literary scholarship, playing upon the messianic rigidity and even bitterness with which ideological and methodological positions are argued while literature itself, the raison d'être of criticism, is totally ignored. Major journals are also playfully jibed. *Tel Quel* (Just as it is), for example, the famous journal of semiology, becomes *Quel Sel* (What salt). The Mexican critic seems particularly victimized. His acceptance of the French semiotician is blind, his vocabulary is even more pretentious, and he is the only scholar cited who defends another rather than advance his own position. Nonetheless, he is the only one to return to the literary work in question, even though he apparently does so unknowingly:

Admirable trabajo heurístico el de Gérard Depardiable, que bien cabe calificar de estructuralógico por su doble riqueza *ur*-semiótica y su rigor conyuntural en un campo tan propicio al mero epifonema. Dejaré que un poeta resuma premonitoriamente estas conquistas textológicas que anuncian ya la parametainfracrítica del futuro.
(An admirable heuristic study, that of Gérard Depardiable, which might well be categorized as structurological because of its double ur-semiotic richness and its conjunctive rigor in a field so propitious for mere epiphonemes. I will let a poet premonitorially sum up these textological conquests that already foretell the parametainfracriticism of the future. [98; 72–73])

Cortázar also directs his barbs at Third World politics. "Un pequeño paraíso" ("A Small Paradise" 81–85; 59–62) tells of a country in which the inhabitants are injected with little goldfishes that swim in their bloodstreams and make them happy. The government provides these injections free of charge. However, because the fish gradually mature and die, the citizens must take special medicine to flush them out of their systems. The government charges twenty dollars for each ampule, which means that it collects millions of dollars a year from its poverty-stricken citizenry. But the people are happy.

In those sections dedicated to Lucas, the character is often a thinly veiled Cortázar. In "Lucas, sus discusiones partidarias" ("Lucas, His Partisan Arguments" 177–80; 137–42) he defends difficult, avant-garde literature against the demands of message-oriented militants, a debate that reflects the polemics the author was involved in throughout his life. Lucas proposes that if writers must stop advancing into new frontiers, then others must stand pat as well. Writers will write only that which is easily understood, but then farmers must also give up their tractors for shovels. A comrade, choked with laughter, proposes such "defenestration" upon a unanimous vote. Lucas immediately votes no (182; 142).

A Certain Lucas is a delightful book, with often serious undertones. As a whole it is less esoteric and seemingly more finished than *Cronopios and Famas*. As one might expect, it continues Cortázar's push into subjects traditionally considered untouchable. In "Lucas, sus pudores" ("Lucas, His Modesty" 153–56; 118–20), for example, the protagonist is mortified by the noises he emits, despite all his efforts to be silent, when he is in the bathroom of a house full of people. He is equally chagrined by the odors he leaves behind for the next occupant. *Lucas* is particularly significant for being the last of Cortázar's truly funny books. Later works are much more somber, much more concerned with imparting a serious social message.

The two remaining major works are more difficult to describe. Saúl Sosnowski calls them "almanacs,"[5] while the author himself suggests both almanac and the term "sponge": "Todo lo que sigue participa lo más posible. . .de esa respiración de la esponja en la que continuamente entran y salen peces de recuerdo, alianzas fulminantes de tiempos y estados y materias que la seriedad, esa señora demasiado escuchada, consideraría inconciliables" (Everything that follows imitates to the degree possible. . .the respiration of a sponge, with the coming and going of fishes of memory, explosive combinations of times and states and materials that seriousness, that all-too-heeded lady, would consider irreconcilable).[6] Almanacs, sponges, collages (as the back cover suggests), or miscellanea, these two works, *Around the Day in*

Eighty Worlds, and *Ultimo round*[7] are among the most innovative and important of Cortázar's works. Each contains a wide variety of literary selections—essays, poems, stories, sketches, and vignettes—as well as photographs, drawings, and reproductions of art works.

The first, *Around the Day*, contains three pieces later included in the complete story collection: "La caricia más profunda" ("The Most Profound Caress"), "Estación de la mano" ("Season of the Hand"), and "Con legítimo orgullo" ("With Justifiable Pride"), all discussed in chapter 2. In addition, many of the essays have also been discussed where relevant to other sections of this study. But several selections from this rather free-flowing mixture of literature, art, jazz, and photography are worthy of special attention here.

"Encuentro con el mal" ("Encounter with Evil" 2: 86–96; 112–17), for example, appears to contain another short story that may have been excluded from the complete collection only because it recounts a "real" episode from Cortázar's life. Here, it is intercalated within a piece on famous murderers. It is less about a confrontation with evil than with fear. The narrator (Cortázar himself?) is riding in a bus with a handful of passengers when a man dressed totally in black gets on. He senses the fear that the ominous stranger inspires in all the passengers (or projects his own fear onto them). What the protagonist dreads happens; the man in black gets off at his stop, but as the narrator scurries off into the dark night he looks over his shoulder to discover that the figure has disappeared.

Another selection, "Noches en los ministerios de Europa" ("Nights in Europe's Ministries" 1:113–19; 47–51), describes the eerie nocturnal reality of official government buildings into which, by means of side entrances, unknown translators, such as Cortázar himself, may enter without even showing identification papers. Within these strongholds of power to which almost everyone including the citizenry is denied access, foreign translators glide up and down corridors by night, translating documents, exploring, and even browsing through files and desks.

Other "creative" sketches highlight the author's playfulness. In "Dos historias zoológicas y otra casi" (Two zoological stories and another almost 1:168–74), he tells of an insecticide salesman who uses a trained mosquito to show the efficacy of his product; the problem of unintelligibility in naval jargon (the "almost" zoological story); and provides a paragraph supposedly written by a chicken: "Con lo que pasa es nosotras exaltante. Rápidamente del posesionadas mundo estamos hurra. Era un inofensivo aparentemente cohete lanzado Cañaveral americanos Cabo por los desde" (With that which happens is us carry away. Quickly of the possessed world we are hurray. It was an inoffensive apparently rocket launched Cañaveral Americans Cape by the from [1:170]). The piece goes on to suggest that the rocket went off course, fell on the chickens, and as a result they have suddenly learned language, mathematics, literature, and a little chemistry—they are still terrible at sports, however. "De otra máquina célibe" ("On Another Bachelor Machine" 1:121–35; 52–61) describes the "rayuelamatic" (hopscotchmatic), a device invented to facilitate the reading of Cortázar's most famous novel. The descriptions and accompanying sketches and diagrams reveal an apparatus that will feed the reader the chapters in the proper order. Deluxe models include a couch, food, drink, and anything else the user may require to read the novel without discomfort or interruption.

Two essays provide valuable insights into the reasons for Cortázar's success as a writer. "No hay peor sordo que el que" (There is no one more deaf than the one who 1:142–59) discusses the reasons for the failure of authors from the River Plate region. Cortázar believes that writers from the area place far too much emphasis on conveying information, on the message, with too little attention to style, arguments reminiscent of his running polemic with socialist critics. The following essay, "Hay que ser realmente idiota para" ("Only a Real Idiot" 1:161–67; 62–65) describes the author's unbridled and unabashed enthusiasm for the creative efforts of others, even when it is undeserved. He admits to being little more than a child in theaters and concert halls, one whose enthusiasm is not shared by wife or friends who are sufficiently intelligent and objective to recognize inferiority. These two essays, the first on the importance of style over content, the second concerning the author's ingenuous delight in art and the world about him, provide important keys to Cortázar's immense success as a creative artist.

Another selection, "El noble arte" (The noble art 2:124–28), which has already been discussed in the context of the author's boxing stories, not only provides an insight into one of his consuming passions, boxing, but a bridge to his other "sponge book," *Ultimo round*. Much has been made of Cortázar's love for jazz, but hardly anything has been written about his equally important enthusiasm for boxing, although references to great fights and fighters are spread liberally throughout his works. *Ultimo round* begins with a very brief poem, followed by a selection entitled "Descripción de un combate o a buen entendedor" (Description of a fight, or to the well-initiated 1:10–14), in which Cortázar describes Juan Yepes's unsuccessful attempt at a comeback. *Ultimo round* is certainly not the author's last round, as the title suggests, nor was he in need of a comeback as a writer, for his international prestige was ever on the rise. However, the boxing analogies suggest that he was keenly aware that a writer, like a prize-fighter, may well deteriorate with time. All of his writings on boxing stress the importance of skill, training, and courage, certainly as important to the writer as to the athlete, and he frequently compared the two professions, even though the writer has no visible opponent. However, as William L. Siemens has pointed out, the description and the photographs that accompany the essay portray only one fighter, the fallen former champion.[8]

Ultimo round is the most interesting and the most important of the potpourri books. In the first edition, even its physical nature was radically different, for the pages were cut horizontally, with one text on the top two-thirds and another on the bottom. The lower pages were in small print and normally contained documents and short texts, while the upper pages contained selections that Cortázar considered more significant.[9] While the typography has been preserved to a degree in subsequent editions, the layout, with its dramatic impact on the reading process, has not. Equally unfortunate is the fact that in later editions the cross-references within the book and the page references provided on the covers of the two volumes were not corrected, but still refer to the original edition, which, although highly recommended, is difficult to find.[10]

Like *Around the Day in Eighty Worlds, Ultimo round* contains a dizzying array of materials: poems, stories, letters, documents, essays, photographs and drawings. Most, but not all, are by Cortázar. The short stories that were later included in the complete collection have been discussed in earlier chapters, as have the essays that deal with the nature of literature, the role of the writer, and politics. Some fictional selections, those that resemble the sketches found in the earlier *Cronopios* and the later *Lucas*, were not included in the story collection, however.

In one, "Los testigos" ("The Witnesses" 1:44–55; *Around the Day* 153–57), the narrator observes a fly that flies upside down. He sections off his apartment, gradually reducing the insect's available space, so that he can observe it close up. Once he has it well confined, he tells his friend Polanco (whom the reader will remember from *62: A Model Kit*) about his discovery, and asks him to verify it. Polanco refuses, on the basis that no one will believe him, for the fly is not upside down at all; the rest of the world has become inverted.[11]

In an equally playful spirit, "El tesoro de la juventud" (The treasure of youth 1:83–87) describes how scientists improve the transportation system through a sort of reverse evolution: the propeller plane is found to be superior to the jet, the ship and the train superior to the propeller plane, and so forth, until the best means of locomotion of all, walking, is finally discovered. In "De la grafología como ciencia aplicada" ("On Graphology as an Applied Science" 2:256–59; *Around the Day* 271–73) Cortázar demonstrates the ramifications of graphology, basing his sketch on the premise that if one's handwriting can reveal everything about his or her character, then one only need learn to write exactly like Napoleon for the process to work in reverse. "Datos para entender a los perqueos" ("Some Facts for Understanding the Perkians" 2:260–64; 274–76) describes how in the country of Perk they invented the wheel, but unlike that of the rest of the world, their version is imperfectly round, having a projection in one spot. These projections result in a sharp jolt with every turn of the wheel, or several jolts if the four wheels on a carriage are not aligned. This phenomenon has had quite notable effects on the Perkian culture, including its perceptions and language.

As delightful as these sketches and others included in the work may be, the essayistic writings are far more significant. As in the case of *Around the Day*, many of the selections in *Ultimo round* are reprinted from elsewhere, but several important pieces appear here for the first time. Martin S. Stabb has pointed out the degree to which the success of these "new essays" depends upon the authorial voice with which each is presented.[12] Cortázar uses six separate voices, ranging from the neutral third person, which establishes a formal distance between author and reader, through the experimental or "Cronopian" voice of the more playful pieces. Because of the dynamic interplay between voice and content, Stabb considers many of the selections treated here as sketches or vignettes, particularly those from *A Certain Lucas*, *Around the Day* and *Ultimo round*, to be essayistic writings.

"Uno de tantos días de Saignon" (One day among many in Saignon 1:16–41) offers a very personal diary of a Thursday at Cortázar's summer home. Interspersed with comments on quotidian activities and the arrival and departure of friends, the author describes his own creative efforts and his deeply felt attitudes on current social issues. The extremely personal, first-person voice gives the text an intimacy and importance it would not otherwise achieve. In "Noticias del mes de mayo" (News for the Month of May 1:88–119), however, the author's voice is absent. Instead, Cortázar presents a collage of graffiti, quotations, poems, slogans, graphic arts, and other miscellaneous "texts" that offer the reader seemingly unmediated insights into Paris's student revolt of May 1968. As usual, despite the serious content, Cortázar's humor is evident: "INVENTEN NUEVAS PERVERSIONES SEXUALES (¡NO PUEDO MÁS!)" ("INVENT NEW SEXUAL PERVERSIONS [I CAN'T TAKE ANY MORE!]" [1:114]).

"Turismo aconsejable" ("Advice for Tourists" 1:123–47; 170–79), on the other hand, is extremely somber. Here Cortázar draws on the distress he suffered at observing first hand the poverty of Calcutta. The prose descriptions of squalor seem objective to the point of indifference, and are accompanied by photographs of the scenes described. Undercutting this "objectivity" of the tourist, who is described in the formal second person, is the irony of his creature comforts—the air-conditioned hotel, the taxi, the desire to see something picturesque—and as he wanders about the misery, after seeing a woman that he soon realizes is dead from hunger and neglect, he observes, "La guía de Murray tiene mucha razón: el espectáculo es pintoresco" ("*Murray's Guide* was quite right: the scene is picturesque" [1:141; 177]). At the teeming Howrah Station, where hordes of the poor live and die in their own filth, he is finally overtaken by nausea. Cortázar, pointing out that he himself has been that tourist, concludes with his most bitter sarcasm: "Algo verdaderamente pintoresco, inolvidable. Vale la pena, le digo" ("Something truly picturesque, unforgettable. It is worth the trouble, believe me" [1:146; 179]).

Ultimo round seems to be simultaneously the author's most playful and most serious book. It is also his most important work in terms of the sensual and the erotic. In "/que sepa abrir la puerta para ir a jugar" (/May you learn to open the door to go out to play 2:58–85) he seriously proposes that the lack of erotica in Latin America is proof of underdevelopment. Advanced, confident cultures, such as those of France, England, and the United States, all have large quantities of erotica. The text, filled with references to and quotes from some of the major works of erotic literature, is accompanied by pictures of the scantily clad lower torso of a woman and by other suggestive illustrations.

The extremely sensual "Tu más profunda piel" ("Your Most Profound Skin" 1:198–203; 196–98) is reminiscent of the love scenes from *A Manual for Manuel* and *62: A Model Kit*. The narrator, whose memories are triggered by the sensuous odor of tobacco, addresses his now-absent lover. Unlike the scenes in the novels, however, this description is purely sensual; the woman is willing and even eager to yield to the narrator's desires. The selection is illustrated by a photograph of a woman's reclining nude body, seen from the waist down and from the rear.

Less obvious, but equally sensual, is Cortázar's description of a girl, perched on the seat of a parked bicycle while engaged in conversation with friends, in "Ciclismo en Grignan" ("Cycling in Grignan" 2:22–26; 218–20). The first-person narrator, enjoying a cup of coffee at a sidewalk café in Grignan, observes and is totally mesmerized by the interaction between the animated young woman's tightly clad buttocks and the leather-covered bicycle seat. Again, while reference is made to sexual intercourse *per angostam viam* (25; 219), unlike in the novels, here the act is not violent. In fact, the heightened eroticism of *Ultimo round* is due primarily to the increased role played by the narrator's, and hence the reader's, imagination.

One of the best selections in this vein, by Cortázar or any other author, is "La noche de Saint-Tropez" ("Saint-Tropez Night" 2:192–96; 250–53), in which the author describes a lush tropical evening. From the perspective of a yacht moored at a busy dock, Cortázar describes the sights, the sounds, and the smells of the evening, as scantily dressed women and eager young men pass by. The center of focus is a Harley Davidson motorcycle parked nearby. All stop to admire it; some even dare to mount it. The cycle, lovingly described, becomes an obvious symbol of sensuality and sexuality. The wave-induced rising and falling of the yacht and the extremely rhythmic prose, simultaneously breathless (it is composed of but one five-page sentence) and panting, combine with the sensual descriptions to make this one of Cortázar's most erotic pieces, though devoid of any description of actual lovemaking.

Also significant in *Ultimo round*, although less important than the selections already discussed, are those pieces that, in true Cortazarian fashion, simply toy with the very bases of literature. "Desayuno" (Breakfast 2:45–47)[13] tells the rather simple story of what happens in the narrator's home on a typical morning—but the nouns and pronouns are all wrong. The narrator says "Good morning, brother" to his mother. "Good morning, Doctor," she replies. He greets his father with "Good morning, nephew" and receives a "Good morning, lover" in return. Language is also undermined in "La inmiscusión terrupta" (Meddlance Tersplat 2:110–11), which is narrated in "giglish," the nonsense language invented by the characters of *Hopscotch*.

"Cortísimo metraje" ("Short Feature" 2:55–56; 232) imitates a film that has been so severely cut that it reads like a sort of shorthand. Nonetheless, the reader is able to piece together the story of a man who picks up a young woman hitchhiker, then tries to rape her. The woman, however, shoots him with a pistol she had hidden, robs him, and steals his car. It is clear that she is a professional highway bandit.

Finally, "Ya no quedan esperanzas de" (There is no hope left that 2:153–65)[14] is comprised of only the introductory clauses for sentences that the reader has to complete. This challenge echoes that offered by the series of poems from volume 1 (276–92), which the reader is instructed to cut into segments (following the dotted lines, of course!), shuffle, and read. While *Ultimo round* is far less radical, it contains an obvious echo of Marc Saporta's *Composition Number 1*.

These works, *Cronopios and Famas, A Certain Lucas, Around the Day in Eighty Worlds,* and *Ultimo round,* as well as other essayistic works such as *Prosa del observatorio, Territorios,* and *Silvalandia,* all discussed in chapter 1, reflect Cortázar's fidelity to the principles he repeatedly defended in his debates with those critics who demanded of him more message and less play. His advice to writers is again clearly and succinctly stated in "No te dejes" ("Don't Let Them" *Ultimo round,* 2:189; *Around the Day* 248): do not let the capitalists buy you out; do not let those who share your views force you away from literature and into dogmatic "commitment"; maintain at all costs that delicate balance that allows your "commitment" to flower in your art. In summary, "Amarga y necesaria moraleja: No te dejes comprar, pibe, pero tampoco vender" ("Bitter but necessary moral: Don't let them buy you out, [kid], but don't sell yourself either"). These works in particular reveal the degree to which Cortázar was successful in pursuing those goals.

Conclusion

Because of the dramatic and enduring impact of *Hopscotch*, not only on Latin American letters, but on an international scale as well, Julio Cortázar's place in literary history seems quite secure. Nonetheless, to consider Cortázar simply as the author of that one work, no matter how significant its influence, is to underestimate his worth severely. When one surveys his brilliant career, one is struck by both the volume and the quality of his achievement.

Surely, when measured by any standard, he must be considered one of the foremost writers of short stories of all time. While *Hopscotch* is undeniably one of the more influential novels of the twentieth century, and perhaps the most influential work of the Latin American "boom," Cortázar clearly had his peers as a novelist. But apart from fellow Argentine Jorge Luis Borges, he seems to have no equal as an author of short stories.

Moreover, his contributions to the development of the "new essay," that peculiar mix of artistic text with the clear communication of ideas, and his attacks against literary texts as rigid artifacts, seen particularly in *Around the Day in Eighty Worlds* and in *Ultimo round*, have had a liberating effect on Latin American letters, the end effects of which may not be measurable for some time to come.

Notes and References

Chapter One

1. *Presencia* (Buenos Aires: Bibliófilo, 1938).
2. "Rimbaud," *Huella* 2 (1941): 7–41.
3. "Casa tomada," *Anales de Buenos Aires* 1, 11 (1946):13–18.
4. *Los reyes* (Buenos Aires: Gulab y Aldabahor, 1949).
5. Louisa May Alcott, *Mujercitas,* trans. Julio Cortázar (Buenos Aires: Codex, 1951).
6. *Bestiario* (Buenos Aires: Sudamericana, 1951).
7. Edgar Allen Poe, *Obras en prosa,* trans. Julio Cortázar (Madrid: Revista de Occidente, 1956).
8. *Final del juego* (México, D.F.: Los Presentes, 1956). A much expanded version was published under the same title in Buenos Aires in 1964.
9. *Las armas secretas* (Buenos Aires: Sudamericana, 1959).
10. "Apocalipsis de Solentiname," *Alguien que anda por ahí* (Madrid: Alfaguara, 1977), 93–105; "Apocalypse at Solentiname," trans. Gregory Rabassa, *We Love Glenda So Much and A Change of Light* (New York: Knopf, 1984), 265–273.
11. Julio Cortázar and Carol Dunlop, *Los autonautas de la cosmopista* (Barcelona: Muchnik, 1984).
12. Omar Prego, *La fascinación de las palabras, conversaciones con Julio Cortázar* (Barcelona: Muchnik, 1985), 184.
13. Ernesto González Bermejo, *Conversaciones con Cortázar* (Barcelona: Edhasa, 1978), 22.
14. Evelyn Picon Garfield, *Cortázar por Cortázar,* 2d. ed. (Xalapa, México: Universidad Veracruzana, 1981), 128.
15. Prego, *Conversaciones,* 165.
16. Luis Harss and Barbara Dohmann, *Into the Mainstream* (New York: Harper & Row, 1967), 229.
17. González Bermejo, *Conversaciones,* 67.
18. *Rayuela* (Buenos Aires: Sudamericana, 1963); *Hopscotch,* trans. Gregory Rabassa (New York: Pantheon, 1966).
19. *62. modelo para armar* (Buenos Aires: Sudamericana, 1968); *62: A Model Kit,* trans. Gregory Rabassa (New York: Pantheon, 1972).
20. Néstor García Canclini, *Cortázar: una antropología poética* (Buenos Aires: Nova, 1968), 62.
21. González Bermejo, *Conversaciones,* 19.
22. Ibid., 148.

23. Rita Guibert, *Seven Voices*, trans. Frances Partridge (New York: Knopf, 1973), 289.

24. Sara de Mundo Lo, *Julio Cortázar, His Works and His Critics: A Bibliography* (Urbana, Ill.: Albatross, 1985).

25. Quoted in Harss and Dohmann, *Mainstream*, 217.

26. *Los reyes* (Madrid: Alfaguara, 1984), 17.

27. *Prosa del observatorio* (Barcelona: Lumen, 1972).

28. Claude Lamotte, *Le Monde* (14 April 1971).

29. Martin S. Stabb, "Not Text but Texture: Cortázar and the New Essay," *Hispanic Review* 52 (1984): 27.

30. *Salvo el crepúsculo* (México, D.F.: Nueva Imagen, 1984).

31. *Libro de Manuel* (Buenos Aires: Sudamericana, 1973); *A Manual for Manuel*, trans. Gregory Rabassa (New York: Pantheon, 1978).

32. *Pameos y meopas* (Barcelona: OCNOS, Editorial Llibres de Sinera, 1971).

33. *Nada a Pehuajó, un acto; Adiós, Robinson* (México, D.F.: Katun, 1984).

34. Julio Cortázar and Julio Silva, *Silvalandia* (Buenos Aires: Argonauta, 1984).

35. *Territorios* (México, D.F.: Siglo Veintiuno, 1978).

36. *Ultimo round* (México, D.F.: Siglo Veintiuno, 1969).

37. *Alguien que anda por allí* (Madrid: Alfaguara, 1977); *A Change of Light and Other Stories*, trans. Gregory Rabassa (New York: Knopf, 1980).

38. *La vuelta al día en ochenta mundos* (México, D.F.: Siglo Veintiuno, 1967); selections from *La vuelta al día* and from *Ultimo round* appear in *Around the Day in Eighty Worlds*, trans. Thomas Christensen (San Francisco: North Point Press, 1986).

39. David William Foster, *Currents in the Contemporary Argentine Novel: Arlt, Mallea, Sábato and Cortázar* (Columbia, Mo.: University of Missouri, 1975), 98.

40. Enrique Anderson Imbert, quoted by David William Foster and Virginia Ramos Foster in *Modern Latin American Literature*, vol. 1 (New York: Frederick Ungar, 1975), 258.

41. For a sampling of reactions, see Foster and Foster, *Modern Latin American Literature*, 258 ff.

42. Ibid., 264.

43. Rodolfo A. Borello, "El último combate de Julio Cortázar," *Cuadernos Hispanoamericanos* 247 (July 1970): 159–64.

44. Carlos Fuentes, *La nueva novela hispanoamericana* (México, D.F.: Joaquín Mortiz, 1969), 73.

45. Ibid., 77.

46. "Los amigos," *El Grillo de Papel* 2, 6 (1960):13. Later included in *Final del juego* (1964).

47. First published in *Revista de la Universidad de México* 18, 8 (April 1964):14–16. Later included in *Todos los fuegos el fuego* (Buenos Aires: Sudameri-

cana, 1966). Available in English in *All Fires the Fire and Other Stories,* trans. Suzanne Jill Levine (New York: Pantheon, 1973).

48. "Casilla del camaleón," *Indice* 221–23 (1967): 9–10. Most readily available in *La vuelta al día en ochenta mundos* (Mexico, 1967). English version, "The Chameleon's Station," *Around the Day in Eighty Worlds.*

49. "Carta a Roberto Fernández Retamar," *Casa de las Américas* 8, 45 (November–December 1967):5–12. Also available as "Acerca de la situación del intelectual latinoamericano" (Concerning the situation of the Latin American intellectual) in *Ultimo round.*

50. "Casilla del camaleón," in *La vuelta al día en ochenta mundos* 21st ed., vol. 2 (México, D.F.: Siglo Veintiuno, 1986), 192. English version in *Around the Day,* 149.

51. "Acerca de la situación del intelectual latinoamericano," in *Ultimo round* 9th ed., vol. 2 (México, D.F.: Siglo Veintiuno, 1985), 270. Subsequent references are to this edition.

52. *Viaje alrededor de una mesa* (Buenos Aires: Rayuela, 1970).

53. Oscar Collazos, Julio Cortázar, and Mario Vargas Llosa, *Literatura en la revolución y revolución en la literatura* (México, D.F.: Siglo Veintiuno 1970).

54. Guibert, *Seven Voices,* 284.

55. Prego, *Conversaciones,* 138.

56. González Bermejo, *Conversaciones,* 126–27.

57. Garfield, *Cortázar por Cortázar,* 26.

58. González Bermejo, *Conversaciones,* 131.

59. Ibid., 132

60. Garfield, *Cortázar por Cortázar,* 49.

61. "La literatura latinoamericana a la luz de la historia contemporanea," *Inti* 10–11 (1979–1980):17.

62. *Nicaragua, tan violentamente dulce* (Managua: Nueva Nicaragua, 1983), 8–17.

63. "Algunos aspectos del cuento," in Mario Benedetti et al., *Literatura y arte nuevo en Cuba* (Barcelona: Estela, 1971), 262. Translation by Evelyn Picon Garfield, *Julio Cortázar* (New York: Ungar, 1975), 12.

64. Jaime Alazraki, *En busca del unicornio: los cuentos de Julio Cortázar* (Madrid: Gredos, 1983), 21.

65. González Bermejo, *Conversaciones,* 42.

66. Ibid., 42.

67. Alazraki, *En busca del unicornio,* 134.

68. David Lagmanovich, ed., *Estudios sobre los cuentos de Julio Cortázar* (Barcelona: Hispam, 1975), 11–19.

69. Alfred Mac Adam, *El individuo y el otro: crítica a los cuentos de Julio Cortázar* (New York: Librería, 1971), 55–60.

70. Mac Adam, for example, points out three basic situations in all of Cortázar's stories: 1) an initial situation in which the reader meets the characters;

2) something unexpected happens; 3) the consequences of the event are revealed. This is essentially the pattern of state of equilibrium, disequilibrium, return to equilibrium, that Todorov observes in every story. See Tzvetan Todorov, *The Poetics of Prose*, trans. Richard Howard (Ithaca, N.Y.: Cornell University, 1977), 111.

71. Quoted in González Bermejo, *Conversaciones*, 142.

72. *Los relatos* (Madrid: Alianza, 1976, 1985), 4 vols.

73. Especially helpful are the discussions by Margaret Gilbert, Menachem Brinker, and Nelson Goodman, in *New Literary History* 14, 2 (Winter 1983):225–76. See also Michel Foucault, "The Prose of the World," in *The Order of Things: An Archaeology of the Human Sciences* (New York: Pantheon, 1970), 17–45, and Roland Barthes, *Image-Music-Text*, trans. Stephen Heath (New York: Hill and Wang, 1977).

74. Todorov, *Poetics of Prose*, 82–83.

75. For a much fuller treatment of this problem, see Terry J. Peavler, *Individuations: The Novel as Dissent* (Landover, Md.: University Press of America, 1987), 5–12.

76. González Bermejo, *Conversaciones*, 47.

77. Quoted in Prego, *Conversaciones*, 60.

78. Ibid., 170

79. Cortázar has described his own creative process in "Del cuento breve y sus alrededores," *Ultimo Round*, 1:59–82. Available in English as "On the Short Story and Its Environs," *Around the Day*, 158–67.

Chapter Two

1. González Bermejo, *Conversaciones*, 28.

2. *La vuelta al día*, 105–10. Available in English in *Around the Day*, 122–25.

3. Juan José Barrientos, "Las palabras mágicas de Cortázar," in Saúl Yurkievich et al., *Coloquio Internacional: lo lúdico y lo fantástico en la obra de Cortázar* (Madrid: Fundamentos, 1986), 63.

4. First published in *Bestiario*. Here quoted in Spanish from *Relatos* 1:277–85; and in English from *Blow-up and Other Stories*, trans. Paul Blackburn (New York: Macmillan, 1974), 35–44.

5. Graciela de Solá, for example, argues that the story is about the creative process, that each rabbit represents a poem, and that the suicide indicates that Cortázar can no longer write poetry (*Julio Cortázar y el hombre nuevo* [Buenos Aires: Sudamericana, 1968], 45). Juan Carlos Curutchet, on the other hand, believes Cortázar has described a case of insanity (*Julio Cortázar o la crítica de la razón pragmática* [Madrid: Nacional, 1972], 22). Lanin A. Gyurko supports the latter view in "Destructive and Ironically Redemptive Fantasy in Cortázar," *Hispania* 56, 4 (December, 1973):989.

6. Alazraki, *En busca del unicornio*, 77.

7. Jaime Alazraki provides an overview of a wide variety of such interpretations in *En busca del unicornio*, 131.

8. Prego, *Conversaciones,* 57.

9. *Relatos* 1:101–116; first published in *Anales de Buenos Aires* in 1947. Published in English in *Blow-up and Other Stories,* 67–84.

10. García Canclini, *Cortázar: una antropología poética,* 21.

11. Solá, *Julio Cortázar,* 49.

12. Prego, *Conversaciones,* 55.

13. *Relatos* 2:53–61; first published in *Final del juego* (1956).

14. Prego, *Conversaciones,* 83.

15. *Relatos* 1:127–38; first published in *Ultimo round.* Available in English in *Around the Day,* 186-95.

16. *Relatos* 1:256–64; first published in *Final del juego* (1964). English version in *Blow-up and Other Stories,* 25–34.

17. *Relatos* 1:176–85; first published in *Octaedro* (Buenos Aires: Sudamericana, 1974). Available in English in *We Love Glenda So Much,* 209–20.

18. *Relatos* 2:118–30; first published in *Bestiario.*

19. For readers not familiar with the theories of *écriture,* which demonstrate that the literary nature of a text derives from its formal characteristics, characteristics that deny the reader access to any specific textual meaning, I recommend David William Foster's *Studies in the Contemporary Spanish-American Short Story* (Columbia, Mo.: University of Missouri, 1979). The first chapter provides a good introduction to the concept of *écriture,* and chapters 6 and 7 deal specifically with texts by Cortázar. While Cortázar's works are masterpieces of *écriture,* I would maintain that they nonetheless reflect, to varying degrees, an external world. My quarrel with many of Cortázar's critics is that they have sought to reduce that referential "meaning" to single interpretations, rather than accomodate the multiplicity of possiblities they demand.

20. *Relatos* 1:169–75; first published in *La vuelta al día en ochenta mundos.* Available in English in *Around the Day,* 76–81.

21. *Relatos* 2:171–80; first published in *Plural* 2 (November 1971):3–6, and included in *Octaedro.* English translation, "Summer," trans. Clementine Rabassa, in *We Love Glenda So Much,* 149–60.

22. *Relatos* 3:35–47; first published in *Queremos tanto a Glenda y otros cuentos* (México, D.F.: Nueva Imagen, 1980). Available in English in *We Love Glenda So Much,* 129–45.

23. González Bermejo, *Conversaciones,* 139.

24. Rosalba Campra, "Fantasma, ¿estás?," in Saúl Yurkievich et al., *Lo lúdico y lo fantástico,* 216.

25. Alicia Helda Puleo, "La sexualidad fantástica," in Yurkievich et al., *Lo lúdico y lo fantástico,* 206–7.

26. *Relatos* 2:284–307; first published in *Todos los fuegos el fuego* (Buenos Aires: Sudamericana, 1966). English version in *All Fires the Fire,* 3–29.

27. In González Bermejo, *Conversaciones,* 57.

28. *Relatos* 3:13–34; first published in *Todos los fuegos el fuego*. English version in *All Fires the Fire*, 128–52.

29. *Relatos* 2:110–17; first published in *Final del juego* (1964). English version available in *Americas* 11 (7 November 1959):24–27.

30. *Relatos* 3:119–43; first published in *Las armas secretas*. English version in *Blow-up and Other Stories*, 221–48.

31. Prego, *Conversaciones*, 82.

32. For an analysis of the story's structure and possible meanings, see Foster, "Cortázar's 'Las armas secretas' and Structurally Anomalous Narratives," in *Spanish-American Short Story*, 83–101.

33. Evelyn Picon Garfield, *Julio Cortázar* (New York: Ungar, 1975), 39–40. The other stories in the collection are "Cartas de Mamá" (Letters from Mama); "Los buenos servicios" ("At Your Service"); "Las babas del diablo" ("Blow-up"); and "El perseguidor" ("The Pursuer"). All but "Cartas de Mamá" are included in *Blow-up and Other Stories*.

34. *Relatos* 2:20–23; first published in *Final del juego* (1964).

35. *Relatos* 1:213–21; *Blow-up* 57–66; first published in *Final del juego* (1956).

36. José Amícola, *Sobre Cortázar* (Argentina: Escuela, 1969), 143.

37. Prego, *Conversaciones*, 65.

38. *Relatos* 2:133–44; first published in *Todos los fuegos el fuego*. English version in *All Fires the Fire*, 114–27.

39. *Relatos* 3:144–51; first published in *Todos los fuegos el fuego*. English version in *All Fires the Fire*, 90–98.

40. Evelyn Picon Garfield, *Cortázar por Cortázar*, 2d. ed. (Xalapa, México: Universidad Veracruzana, 1981), 15.

41. Harss and Dohmann, *Into the Mainstream*, 224.

42. *Relatos* 3:90–98; first published in *Bestiario*. English version in *Blow-up*, 15–24.

43. Curutchet, *La razón pragmática*, 37.

44. Mac Adam, *El individuo y el otro*, 58.

45. Alazraki, *En busca del unicornio*, 205.

46. Garfield, *Cortázar por Cortázar*, 92.

47. *Relatos* 1:200–205; first published in *Buenos Aires Literaria* 3 (1954), and included in *Final del juego* (1956). English version in *Blow-up*, 3–8.

48. Mac Adam, for example, argues that the story is a metaphor for the impossibility of communication (*El individuo y el otro*, 101).

49. *Relatos* 3:83–89; first published in *Revista de Occidente* 2,6 (1963), and included in *Final del juego* (1964). English version in *Blow-up*, 45–52.

50. For fuller explanations of the concept of a covert first-person narrator, see Robert Scholes, *Semiotics and Interpretation* (New Haven: Yale University Press, 1982), chapter 7 and Terry J. Peavler, *El texto en llamas: el arte narrativo de Juan Rulfo* (New York: Peter Lang, 1988), chapter 2. For an excellent treatment of narra-

tors and narratees see Gérard Genette, *Narrative Discourse: An Essay in Method* (Ithaca: Cornell University Press, 1980), chapter 5.

51. *Relatos* 3:205–19; first published in *Las armas secretas*. English version in *Blow-up*, 100–115.

52. For a much fuller analysis of this story, see Terry J. Peavler, "*Blow-up:* A Reconsideration of Antonioni's Infidelity to Cortázar," *PMLA* 94, no. 5 (October 1979):887–93.

53. This point is developed at length in Peavler, "Antonioni's Infidelity."

54. *Relatos* 4:12–18; first published in *Alguien que anda por allí*. English version in *We Love Glenda So Much*, 265–73.

55. *Relatos* 1:50–59; first published in *Deshoras* (Madrid: Alfaguara, 1982).

56. The details of Dalton's death on 10 May 1975 may never be known. At first, the CIA was proported to have been involved, but Dalton's friend and translator, Margaret Randall, believes he was tortured and killed by a "militaristic faction of his own organization," who then blamed the CIA. Cortázar undoubtedly believed the CIA was involved. See Margaret Randall's introduction to Roque Dalton, *Poemas clandestinos/Clandestine Poems* (San Francisco: Solidarity Publications, 1984), x.

57. Malva E. Filer, "El texto, espacio de la vida y de la muerte en los últimos cuentos de Julio Cortázar," in Saúl Yurkievich et al., *Lo lúdico y lo fantástico*, 225–32.

58. Jaime Alazraki, "Los últimos cuentos de Julio Cortázar," *Revista Iberoamericana* 51, 130–31 (January–June 1985): 31–32.

59. *Relatos* 2:181–94; first published in *Marcha* (25 June 1965), and included in *Todos los fuegos el fuego*, English version in *All Fires the Fire*, 99–113.

60. *Relatos* 2:7–8; originally published in *El Grillo del Papel* (1960) and included in *Final del juego* (1964), English version in *Blow-up*, 55–56.

61. González Bermejo, *Conversaciones*, 104.

62. *Relatos* 2:266–75; first published in *Queremos tanto a Glenda y otros relatos*, English version in *We Love Glenda So Much*, 116–28.

Chapter Three

1. *Relatos*, 1:60–74; first published in *Bestiario*.

2. Prego, *Conversaciones*, 182–83.

3. Alazraki, *En busca del unicornio*, 238.

4. Ana Hernández del Castillo has made an excellent study of women in Cortázar's works, and discusses how he was influenced by other writers in their portrayal. The Circe myth was drawn from Keats. See Hernández del Castillo, *Cortázar's Mythopoesis*, Purdue University Monographs in Romance Languages, 8 (Amsterdam: J. Benjamin, 1981).

5. *Relatos* 3:99–103; first published in *Final del juego* (1956).

6. Jaime Alazraki, "Los últimos cuentos," 27.

7. Garfield, *Cortázar por Cortázar*, 107.

8. *Relatos* 2:105–9; first published in *Final del juego* (1964).

9. *Relatos* 1:222–29; originally published in *Alguien que anda por ahí*. Available in English in *We Love Glenda So Much*, 299–308.

10. González Bermejo, *Conversaciones*, 144.

11. *Relatos* 1:295–99; first published in *Queremos tanto a Glenda*. Available in English in *We Love Glenda So Much*, 3–7.

12. *Relatos* 1:299–306; first published in *Queremos tanto a Glenda*. Available in English in *We Love Glenda So Much*, 8–16.

13. *Relatos* 1:307–12; first published in *Deshoras*.

14. *Relatos* 1:139–48; First published in *Alguien que anda por ahí*. Available in English in *We Love Glenda So Much*, 393–404.

15. *Relatos* 2:242–59; first published in *Queremos tanto a Glenda*. Available in English in *We Love Glenda So Much*, 39–59.

16. *Relatos* 2:308–14; first published in *Final del juego* (1956).

17. *Relatos* 1:206–12; first published in *Final del juego* (1964).

18. Hernández del Castillo, *Cortázar's Mythopoesis*, 120, note 26.

19. *Relatos* 2:62–75; first published in *Octaedro* (Buenos Aires; Sudamericana 1974). Available in English in *We Love Glenda So Much*, 405–21.

20. Rosalba Campra, "Fantasma, ¿estás?," 219.

21. *Relatos* 1:36–49; first published in *Queremos tanto a Glenda*. Available in English in *We Love Glenda So Much*, 60–77.

22. *Relatos* 2:315–42; first published in *Deshoras*.

23. Prego, *Conversaciones*, 38.

24. Alazraki, "Los últimos cuentos," 45.

25. Prego, *Conversaciones*, 37.

26. *Relatos* 2:34–52; first published in *Octaedro*. Available in English in *We Love Glenda So Much*, 275–97.

27. *Relatos* 1:75–86; first published in *Octaedro*. Available in English in *We Love Glenda So Much*, 249–63.

28. González Bermejo, *Conversaciones*, 46.

29. *Relatos* 1:286–94; first published in *Alguien que anda por ahí*. Available in English in *We Love Glenda So Much*, 237–47.

30. *Relatos* 4:82–91; first published in *Deshoras*.

31. Alazraki, "Los últimos cuentos," 40.

32. *Relatos* 4:61–81.

33. Alazraki, points out that Nito has been taken in by the blind obedience to power in Argentina, and should be read as "argentinito" (the little Argentine). See "Los últimos cuentos," 36.

34. Prego, *Conversaciones*, 177.

35. *Relatos* 3:48–82; first published in *Alguien que anda por ahí*. Available in English in *We Love Glenda So Much*, 335–79.

36. Monique J. Lemaître has analysed Dora's contributions to the story in "Cortázar en busca de uno de sus personajes," *Revista Iberoamericana* 44, 102–3 (January–June 1978):139–46.

37. *Relatos* 2:24–33; first published in *Queremos tanto a Glenda*. Available in English in *We Love Glenda So Much*, 17–29.

38. *Relatos* 1:117–26; first published in *Final del juego* (1964).

39. *Relatos* 2:156–70; first published in *Queremos tanto a Glenda*. Available in English in *We Love Glenda So Much*, 97–115.

40. *Relatos* 1:230–55; first published in *Las armas secretas*. Available in English in *Blow-up and Other Stories*, 132–60.

41. Alazraki, *En busca del unicornio*, 238.

42. Garfield, *Julio Cortázar*, 45.

Chapter Four

1. For a full development of these readings and many others, see Lanin A. Gyurko, "Destructive and Ironically Redemptive Fantasy in Cortázar," *Hispania* 56, 4 (December 1973):988–99.

2. See, for example, Curutchet, *Crítica de la razón pragmática*, 23.

3. Alazraki, *En busca del unicornio*, 205.

4. *Relatos* 3:182–94; first published in *Bestiario*. Available in English in *Blow-up and Other Stories*, 85–99.

5. Alazraki, *En busca del unicornio*, 238.

6. Garfield, *Cortázar por Cortázar*, 97.

7. *Relatos* 1:265–76; originally published in *Final del juego* (1956). English version in *Blow-up*, 119–31.

8. *Relatos* 2:76–89; first published in *Final del juego* (1956).

9. Gonzáles Bermejo, *Conversaciones*, 51.

10. *Relatos* 2:207–27; first published in *Todos los fuegos el fuego*. Available in English in *All Fires the Fire*, 65–89.

11. *Relatos* 1:87–100; first published in *Ultimo round*. The translation in *Around the Day in Eighty Worlds*, 277–88, is not recommended. Key passages are either mistranslated or omitted altogether.

12. Lanin A. Gyurko believes the paintings are by Delvaux. See "Art and the Demonic in Three Stories by Cortázar," *Symposium* 37, 1 (Spring 1983):14–47.

13. Gyurko, "Destructive and Ironically Redemptive Fantasy," 990.

14. "Cartas de mamá," *Relatos* 1:7–25; first published in *Americas* 11, 2 (1959), and later included in *Las armas secretas*. "La salud de los enfermos," *Relatos* 3:152–67; first published in *Todos los fuegos el fuego*. In English in *All Fires the Fire*, 30–48. "Las ménades," *Relatos* 1:186–99; first published in *Final del juego* (1956).

15. Jaime Alazraki, "From *Bestiary* to *Glenda*: Pushing the Short Story to Its Utmost Limits," *Review of Contemporary Fiction* 3, 3 (Fall 1983):94.

16. Elvira Aguirre, "Libertad condicional o el problema de la subjetividad en la obra de Julio Cortázar," in Saúl Yurkievich et al., *Lo lúdico y lo fantástico*, 127.

17. *Relatos* 3:220–74; first published in *Las armas secretas*. Available in English in *Blow-up and Other Stories*, 161–220.

18. Lanin A. Gyurko, "Artist and Critic as Self and Double in Cortázar's 'Los pasos en las huellas,'" *Hispania* 65, 3 (September 1982):354.

19. Robert W. Felkel, "The Historical Dimension in Julio Cortázar's 'The Pursuer,'" *Latin American Literary Review* 71, 14 (Spring–Summer 1979): 20–27.

20. Prego, *Conversaciones*, 67.

21. Ibid., 130.

22. See, for example, Curutchet, *Crítica de la razón pragmática*, especially pages 25 and 46.

23. Garfield, *Julio Cortázar*, 47.

24. García Canclini, *Cortázar: una antropología poética*, 66.

25. *Relatos* 2:145–55; first published in *Ultimo round*. Available in English in *Around the Day*, 221–29.

26. Evelyn Picon Garfield, "*Octaedro*: Eight Phases of Despair," in Jaime Alazraki and Ivar Ivask, eds., *The Final Island: The Fiction of Julio Cortázar* (Norman: University of Oklahoma Press, 1978), 115–28.

27. Ibid., 126.

28. Marta Morello-Frosch, "*Octaedro*: o los puentes circulares," *Revista Hispánica Moderna* 39, 4 (1977):198–209.

29. Ibid., 127.

30. *Relatos* 3:195–204; first published in *Octaedro*. Available in English in *We Love Glenda So Much*, 381–92.

31. *Relatos* 1:26–35; first published in *Crisis* 1, 11 (March 1974). English version in *We Love Glenda So Much*, 173–83.

32. González Bermejo, *Conversaciones*, 56–57.

33. *Relatos* 2:9–19; originally published in *Libre* 1 (1971). Available in English in *We Love Glenda So Much*, 185–98.

34. Garfield, "Eight Phases of Despair," 124.

35. Gyurko, "Artist and Critic as Self and Double," 362.

36. *Relatos* 2:90–99. This story is the only selection from *Alguien que anda por ahí* that was omitted from the collection *We Love Glenda So Much*. Its exclusion is probably due to the difficulty in effectively translating the verbal play on the formal and the informal "you" ("usted" and "vos").

37. González Bermejo, *Conversaciones*, 146.

38. *Relatos* 1:160–68; first published in *Alguien que anda por ahí*. Available in English in *We Love Glenda So Much*, 161–71.

39. *Relatos* 3:168–81; first published in *Alguien que anda por ahí*. Available in English in *We Love Glenda So Much*, 309–25.

40. Alicia Helda Puleo, "La sexualidad fantástica," in Yurkievich et al., *Lo lúdico y lo fantástico*, 212.

41. Alazraki, "Los últimos cuentos de Julio Cortázar," 38.

42. Ibid., 39.

Chapter Five

1. *Relatos* 2:276–83; first published in *Final del juego* (1956).
2. *Relatos* 2:131–32; first published in *El Grillo de Papel* 2, 6 (1960):13.
3. In *La vuelta al día en ochenta mundos* 2:124–28.
4. In *Ultimo round* 1:10–14.
5. Luis Leal, "Situación de Julio Cortázar," *Revista Iberoamericana* 39, 84–85 (July–December 1973):399–409.
6. Garfield, *Julio Cortázar,* 35.
7. Mercedes Rein, *Julio Cortázar: el escritor y sus máscaras* (Montevideo: Diaco, 1967), 23.
8. *Relatos* 2:195–206; first published in *Deshoras.*
9. Juan José Barrientos believes the first Argentine boxer to go to the United States only to be defeated, as described in "Segundo viaje," was Luis Angel Firpo, and that the second, who became the protagonist in the story, was Suárez. See Juan José Barrientos, "Las palabras mágicas de Cortázar," in Saúl Yurkievich et al., *Lo lúdico y lo fantástico,* 66.
10. *Relatos* 4:92–104; first published in *Alguien que anda por ahí.* Available in English in *We Love Glenda So Much,* 221–35.
11. *Relatos* 3:104–18; first published in *Todos los fuegos el fuego.* English translation in *All Fires the Fire,* 49–64.
12. See, for example, Curutchet, *Crítica de la razón pragmática,* 140.
13. González Bermejo, *Conversaciones,* 143.
14. Ernesto Che Guevara, *Obras: 1957–1967* vol. 1 (Havana: Casa de las Américas, 1970), 199–200.
15. Mac Adam, *El individuo y el otro,* 139.
16. García Canclini, *Cortázar: una antropología poética,* 77.
17. *Relatos* 4:54–60; first published in *Alguien que anda por ahí.* English translation in *We Love Glenda So Much,* 327–34.
18. *Relatos* 4:19–26; first published in *Alguien que anda por ahí.* Available in English in *We Love Glenda So Much,* 199–207.
19. González Bermejo, *Conversaciones,* 144.
20. *Relatos* 4:7–11; first published in *Queremos tanto a Glenda.* Available in English in *We Love Glenda So Much,* 33–38.
21. Prego, *Conversaciones,* 14.
22. *Relatos* 4:40–53; first published in *Deshoras.*
23. Prego, *Conversaciones,* 37.
24. Alazraki, "Los últimos cuentos," 34.
25. *Relatos* 4:27–39; originally published in *Queremos tanto a Glenda.* Available in English in *We Love Glenda So Much,* 81–96.

Chapter Six

1. Garfield, *Julio Cortázar,* 35.

2. González Bermejo, *Conversaciones*, 86.

3. Harss and Dohmann, *Into the Mainstream*, 216.

4. Harss and Dohmann state that *El examen* was written after *Los premios* (*The Winners*), Cortázar's first published novel. If that is true, *The Winners* languished unpublished for over a decade. See *Into the Mainstream*, 224.

5. *El examen* (Buenos Aires: Sudamericana, 1986), 200.

6. Hernández del Castillo, *Cortázar's Mythopoesis*, 61.

7. *Los premios* (Buenos Aires: Sudamericana, 1960). I have used the sixth edition, published in 1967. Translated into English by Elaine Kerrigan as *The Winners* (New York: Pantheon, 1965).

8. Garfield, *Cortázar por Cortázar*, 112–14.

9. Harss and Dohmann, *Into the Mainstream*, 224–27.

10. Prego, *Conversaciones*, 86.

11. Moreover, Gregory Rabassa's masterful translation launched his stellar career as a translator.

12. *Rayuela* (Buenos Aires: Sudamericana, 1963). The edition quoted here is the fourteenth (1972). The English translation by Gregory Rabassa was first published by Random House (New York) in 1966. The edition used for this study is from Plume Books (New York), 1971.

13. Alazraki, *En busca del unicornio*, 100–101.

14. Saúl Sosnowski, *Julio Cortázar: una búsqueda mítica* (Buenos Aires: Noe, 1973), 121.

15. González Bermejo, *Conversaciones*, 78.

16. Garfield, *Julio Cortázar*, 106.

17. Harss and Dohmann, *Into the Mainstream*, 233.

18. Hernández del Castillo, *Cortázar's Mythopoesis*, 80.

19. Boldy, for example, suggests: 1) madness; 2) suicide; 3) Oliveira plans to go to a film with Gekrepten, in Stephen Boldy, *The Novels of Julio Cortázar* (Cambridge: Cambridge University Press, 1980), 89.

20. Robert Brody, *Julio Cortázar: "Rayuela"* (London: Grant & Cutler, 1976), 37.

21. Ibid., 38.

22. González Bermejo, *Conversaciones*, 74–75.

23. Ibid., 73.

24. See, for example, Kathleen Genover, *Claves de una novelística existencial en "Rayuela" de Cortázar* (Madrid: Playor, 1973), 33.

25. Genover, *Claves de una novelística*, 208.

26. Boldy, *Novels of Julio Cortázar*, 83.

27. Ibid., 21.

28. Prego, *Conversaciones*, 118.

29. Boldy, *Novels of Julio Cortázar*, 8.

30. González Bermejo, *Conversaciones*, 33.

31. Prego, *Conversaciones,* 109.

32. Ibid., 119.

33. Ibid., 110.

34. Ibid., 103.

35. Ibid., 107–8.

36. Brody, *"Rayuela,"* 83.

37. Garfield, *Julio Cortázar,* 105.

38. Harss and Dohmann, *Into the Mainstream,* 218.

39. Brody, *"Rayuela,"* 31.

40. Harss and Dohmann, *Into the Mainstream,* 244.

41. Curutchet, *Crítica de la razón pragmática.* 107.

42. Boldy, *Novels of Julio Cortázar,* 97.

43. Prego, *Conversaciones,* 93–94.

44. *62. modelo para armar* (Buenos Aires: Sudamericana, 1968) 7; *62: A Model Kit,* trans. Gregory Rabassa (New York: Avon, 1973), 7.

45. Garfield, *Julio Cortázar,* 122–23.

46. Ibid., 80.

47. Ibid., 128–29.

48. González Bermejo, *Conversaciones,* 89–90.

49. Prego, *Conversaciones,* 111.

50. These passages and motifs refer to Alejandra Pizarnik's *La condesa sangrienta,* an underground classic in Argentina at the time. Pizarnik's book, in turn, was inspired by Valentine Penrose's *Erzébet Bathory: La Comtesse Sanglante.* Cortázar was probably familiar with both works.

51. Prego, *Conversaciones,* 93.

52. Garfield, *Cortázar por Cortázar,* 109.

53. Garfield, *Julio Cortázar,* 116.

54. Jaime Alazraki, "Introduction: Toward the Last Square of the Hopscotch," in Jaime Alazraki and Ivar Ivask, eds., *The Final Island,* 15.

55. *Libro de Manuel* (Buenos Aires: Sudamericana, 1973). I have used the Bruguera edition (Barcelona, 1983). Translated by Gregory Rabassa as *A Manual for Manuel* (New York: Pantheon, 1978).

56. *Joda* is a taboo word for "bother" or "annoyance." It apparently derives from the verb *joder,* "to fuck"—in the figurative sense. Rabassa translates it as "The Screwery."

57. Prego, *Conversaciones,* 86.

58. Garfield, *Julio Cortázar,* 139–40.

59. Garfield, *Cortázar por Cortázar,* 30.

60. Garfield, *Julio Cortázar,* 138.

61. Garfield, *Cortázar por Cortázar,* 57, 62.

62. Ibid., 30.

63. Boldy, *Novels of Julio Cortázar,* 161.

64. David P. Gallegher, *Modern Latin American Literature* (London: Oxford University Press, 1973), 88–89.

65. Prego, *Conversaciones*, 92.

Chapter Seven

1. *Historias de cronopios y de famas* (Buenos Aires: Minotauro, 1962). I have used the Edhasa edition (Barcelona, 1984). Translated by Paul Blackburn as *Cronopios and Famas* (New York: Pantheon, 1969).

2. For a detailed study of Cortázar's attack on conventional language and de-familiarization of ordinary objects and events, see David William Foster, "The *Écriture* of Rupture and Subversion of Language in Cortázar's *Historias de cronopios y famas*," in David William Foster, *Studies in the Contemporary Spanish-American Short Story* (Columbia, Mo.: University of Missouri, 1979), 63–82.

3. The English version of *Cronopios and Famas* includes several pieces that are not in any of the Spanish editions. They are: "Instructions on How to Comb the Hair," "Instructions on How to Dissect a Ground Owl," "The Prisoner," "The Public Highways," and "Never Stop the Presses." Evidently, Cortázar gave these additional selections to Paul Blackburn while he was working on the translation.

4. *Un tal Lucas* (Madrid: Alfaguara, 1979). I have used the 1984 edition. Translated by Gregory Rabassa as *A Certain Lucas* (New York: Knopf, 1984).

5. Saúl Sosnowski, "Julio Cortázar: modelos para desarmar," in Reina Roffé, ed., *Espejo de escritores: entrevistas con Borges, Cortázar, Fuentes, Goytisolo, Onetti, Puig, Rama, Rulfo, Sánchez, Vargas Llosa* (Hanover, N.H.: Ediciones del Norte, 1985), 58.

6. *La vuelta al día en ochenta mundos*, 1:7 (México, D.F.: Siglo Veintiuno, 1986), 7; my translation. First published in 1967. The translation, *Around the Day in Eighty Worlds*, by Thomas Christensen (San Francisco: North Point, 1986), combines texts selected from *La vuelta al día* and from *Ultimo round*, the author's other "sponge" book. Unfortunately, the translations are often awkward, and at times even inaccurate.

7. *Ultimo round* (México, D.F.: Siglo Veintiuno, 1969). The edition cited here is the tenth, 1986, in two volumes.

8. William L. Siemens, "Cortázar's *Ultimo Round:* A Bi-Level Literary-Pictorial Experience," *International Fiction Review*, 2 (1975):74–77.

9. Evelyn Picon Garfield, *Cortázar por Cortázar*, 2d ed. (Xalapa, México: Universidad Veracruzana, 1981), 47. In this interview, Cortázar also explains that the idea for the layout of the book was Julio Silva's.

10. The first edition was Julio Cortázar, *Ultimo round* (México, D.F.: Siglo Veintiuno, 1969). The most readily available version is the "bolsillo," or pocket edition. My references are to the tenth edition, 1986.

11. "Los testigos," 1: 44–55. Unfortunately, the translation of the story is badly botched. Instead of the world being inverted, the translator has the fly making "half a turn, that's all" (*Around the Day in Eighty Worlds*, 157).

12. Martin S. Stabb, "Not Text but Texture: Cortázar and the New Essay," *Hispanic Review* 52, 1 (Winter 1984):19–40.

13. Christensen translates the title as "Lunch" in *Around the Day*, 230–31.

14. Christensen's version of this piece is "It is Regrettable That" (*Around the Day*, 239–43).

Selected Bibliography

PRIMARY WORKS

Because of space considerations, only selected book-length studies and collections are included. The most current and complete bibliography is Sarah de Mundo Lo, *Julio Cortázar, His Works and His Critics: A Bibliography* (Urbana, Ill.: Albatross, 1985).

Short Story Collections

Los relatos. 4 vols. Madrid: Alianza, 1976–85.
All Fires the Fire and Other Stories. Translated by Jill Levine. New York: Pantheon, 1973.
Blow-up and Other Stories. Translated by Paul Blackburn. New York: Macmillan, 1967.
We Love Glenda So Much and A Change of Light. Translated by Gregory Rabassa. New York: Vintage, 1984.

Novels

Divertimento. Buenos Aires: Sudamericana, 1986.
El examen. Buenos Aires: Sudamericana, 1986.
Libro de Manuel. Barcelona: Bruguera, 1983. *A Manual for Manuel.* Translated by Gregory Rabassa. New York: Pantheon, 1978.
Los premios. Buenos Aires: Sudamericana, 1967. *The Winners.* Translated by Elaine Kerrigan. New York: Pantheon, 1965.
62. modelo para armar. Buenos Aires: Sudamericana, 1968. *62: A Model Kit.* Translated by Gregory Rabassa. New York: Avon, 1972.
Rayuela. Buenos Aires: Sudamericana, 1972. *Hopscotch.* Translated by Gregory Rabassa. New York: Plume, 1971.

Miscellanea

Historias de cronopios y de famas. Barcelona: Edhasa, 1984. *Cronopios and Famas.* Translated by Paul Blackburn. New York: Pantheon, 1969.
Ultimo round. 2 vols. México, D.F.: Siglo Veintiuno, 1985.
Un tal Lucas. Madrid: Alfaguara, 1984. *A Certain Lucas.* Translated by Gregory Rabassa. New York: Knopf, 1984.
Vampiros multinacionales: una utopía realizable. México, D.F.: Excelsior, 1975.

Cover title is *Fantomas contra los vampiros multinacionales,* etc. Includes appendix on Russell Tribunal investigation of crimes against peoples.

La vuelta al día en ochenta mundos. 2 vols. México, D.F.: Siglo Veintiuno, 1970. *Around the Day in Eighty Worlds.* Translated by Thomas Christensen. San Francisco: North Point, 1986. Includes selections from *La vuelta al día* and from *Ultimo round.*

SECONDARY WORKS

Books

Alazraki, Jaime. *En busca del unicornio, los cuentos de Julio Cortázar: elementos para una poética de lo neofantástico.* Madrid: Gredos, 1983. Perhaps the best overall study of Cortázar's stories. Does not include some later works.

Alazraki, Jaime, and Ivar Ivask, eds. *The Final Island: The Fiction of Julio Cortázar.* Norman, Okla.: University of Oklahoma Press, 1978. Excellent collection of essays by some of the best critics of Cortázar's work.

Amícola, José. *Sobre Cortázar.* Argentina: Escuela, 1969. Relatively early study of novels and stories. One of first to discuss novel *El examen,* which was not published until after Cortázar's death.

Boldy, Stephen. *The Novels of Julio Cortázar.* Cambridge: Cambridge University Press, 1980. Only book-length, in-depth study of all of Cortázar's novels. Many valuable insights.

Brody, Robert. *Julio Cortázar: "Rayuela."* Critical Guides to Spanish Texts. London: Grant & Cutler, 1976. Helpful study guide, in English, to Cortázar's most famous work.

Burgos, Fernando, ed. *Los ochenta mundos de Cortázar.* Madrid: Edi-6, 1987. Twenty-two essays by different critics. I was unable to consult this work.

Coloquio internacional: lo lúdico y lo fantástico en la obra de Cortázar. Madrid: Espiral Hispanoamericana, Centre de Recerches Latino-Americaines, Université de Poitiers, 1986. Collection of recent and excellent essays that include discussions of Cortázar's last works.

Curutchet, Juan Carlos. *Julio Cortázar o la crítica de la razón pragmática.* Madrid: Editora Nacional, 1972. In-depth analyses of many stories and novels. Prefers single interpretations for most stories. Eclectic taste in his evaluations of many works.

García Canclini, Néstor. *Cortázar: una antropología poética.* Buenos Aires: Nova, 1968. One of earliest and best studies available. What it covers, it covers extremely well.

Garfield, Evelyn Picon. *Cortázar por Cortázar.* 2d ed. Xalapa, México: Universidad Veracruzana, 1981. Interviews upon which *Julio Cortázar* was based (see following entry). Good, helpful interviews.

_____. *Julio Cortázar.* New York: Frederick Ungar, 1975. One of few books on Cortázar in English. Good overview. Based on series of interviews with Cortázar. Particularly valuable because few of Cortázar's interviews are available in English.

_____. *¿Es Julio Cortázar un surrealista?* Madrid: Gredos, 1975. The answer to the title question is no, he is not a surrealist, but he has much in common with surrealism.

Genover, Kathleen. *Claves de una novelística existencial en "Rayuela" de Cortázar.* Madrid: Playor, 1973. Studies relationship between existential novel and *Rayuela.* Sees *Rayuela* as being removed from the pessimism of early existentialists.

Giacoman, Helmy F., ed. *Homenaje a Julio Cortázar: variaciones interpretativas en torno a su obra.* New York: Las Américas, 1972. Collection of essays by various scholars. Many essays reprinted from elsewhere.

González Bermejo, Ernesto. *Conversaciones con Cortázar.* Barcelona: Edhasa, 1978. One of three extremely valuable series of interviews with Cortázar. See also, Garfield, *Cortázar por Cortázar,* and Prego, *La fascinación de las palabras.* Cortázar discusses works at great length.

Guibert, Rita. *Seven Voices: Seven Latin American Writers Talk to Rita Guibert.* Translated by Frances Partridge, 277-302. New York: Knopf, 1973. Guibert's interview with Cortázar was written out and first published in *Life.* Since Cortázar views his audience as U.S. readers, he takes the opportunity to lecture them on U.S. interference in Latin America, but also discusses many of his works.

Harss, Luis, and Barbara Dohmann. *Into the Mainstream: Conversations with Latin-American Writers,* 206–45. New York: Harper & Row, 1967. Early interviews, but still useful, particularly for those who cannot read Spanish.

Hernández del Castillo, Ana. *Keats, Poe, and the Shaping of Cortázar's Mythopoesis.* Purdue University Monographs in Romance Languages, 8. Amsterdam: J. Benjamin, 1981. Excellent study that explores, in addition to the influence of Keats and Poe, myth in Cortázar. Analyses impressed Cortázar with their rigor and insights.

Lagmanovich, David, ed. *Estudios sobre los cuentos de Julio Cortázar.* Barcelona: Hispam, 1975. Collection of essays by numerous scholars on Cortázar's stories.

Mac Adam, Alfred. *El individuo y el otro: crítica a los cuentos de Julio Cortázar.* New York: Librería, 1971. Originally a doctoral thesis. Divides stories into basic story models. Some good insights, but also some troublesome readings.

Mora Valcárcel, Carmen de. *Teoría y práctica del cuento en los relatos de Julio Cortázar.* Sevilla: Escuela de Estudios Hispano-Americanos, no. 278, 1982. Applies a wide variety of contemporary literary theories to Cortázar's stories with mixed success.

Planells, Antonio. *Cortázar: metafísica y erotismo.* Madrid: Porrúa Turanzas, 1979. Not consulted.

Prego, Omar. *La fascinación de las palabras. Conversaciones con Julio Cortázar.* Barcelona: Muchnik, 1985. Another excellent series of informative interviews with Cortázar. Because of its date, includes discussion of materials published after interviews by Garfield and González Bermejo.

Rein, Mercedes. *Julio Cortázar: el escritor y sus máscaras.* Montevideo: Diaco, 1967. One of earliest lengthy studies. Widely quoted, but has been largely supplanted by subsequent works.

Roy, Joaquín. *Julio Cortázar ante su sociedad.* Barcelona: Península, 1974. On Cortázar and his relationship with Argentina, including how he portrays the country in his work.

Solá, Graciela de. *Julio Cortázar y el hombre nuevo.* Buenos Aires: Sudamericana, 1968. Relatively early study of Cortázar's works. Each story has a single and, according to the author, correct interpretation, some inventive, some insightful.

Sosnowski, Saúl. *Julio Cortázar: una búsqueda mítica.* Buenos Aires: Noé, 1973. Analyses of early stories, *Los premios,* and *Rayuela.*

La vuelta a Cortázar en nueve ensayos. Buenos Aires: C. Pérez, 1968. Nine essays by different scholars on various works.

Special Issues of Journals Dedicated to Cortázar

Books Abroad 50, no. 3 (Summer 1976). Excellent collection of essays by some of Cortázar's best critics. In English.

Cuadernos Hispanoamericanos 364–66 (October–December 1980). Large collection of essays on and reactions to Cortázar's works.

Inti. Revista de Literatura Hispánica 10–11 (Fall 1979–Spring 1980). Includes the proceedings of the symposium on Cortázar held at Barnard College in 1980.

Review. Focus on Julio Cortázar (Winter 1972). Essays, interviews, miscellany on Cortázar. In English.

Revista Iberoamericana 39, no. 84–85 (July–December 1973). Works on and by Cortázar. Twenty-two selections.

Review of Contemporary Fiction 3, no. 3 (Fall 1983). Late collection of essays on Cortázar. Includes interview with author and several essays on Cortázar's last works. Some of Cortázar's best critics represented.

Index

Asterisks indicate translations of titles of works not yet published in English